YORKSHIRE C

YORKSHIRE COTTAGE

Ella Pontefract & Marie Hartley

Dalesman Books
1984

The Dalesman Publishing Company Ltd.,
Clapham, via Lancaster, LA2 8EB

First published by J.M. Dent & Sons Ltd., 1942
Reprinted 1942, 1943, 1947
Re-issued 1977
First paperback edition 1984

ISBN: 0 85206 801 8

Cover photograph by Marie Hartley

Printed by Galava Printing Company Limited, Nelson, Lancashire

CONTENTS

ILLUSTRATIONS

YORKSHIRE COTTAGE or Coleshouse to give it its old name was bought by Ella Pontefract and Marie Hartley in 1938 with a view to living there and continuing their partnership as author and artist in the writing of books. Then almost derelict, the cottage was altered and restored in the months before the outbreak of the Second World War and was completed in the autumn of 1939. The book **Yorkshire Cottage,** describing the renovation and life there, was published in 1942 and became a best seller. The location in the dales was not given, but very many people found it out. It was alas to be Ella Pontefract's last book for she died in 1945.

Since then Joan Ingilby has joined Marie Hartley and they still live in the cottage continuing the partnership of writing books on the dales and Yorkshire. The outside appearance of the cottage from the front is unchanged, but a work room to house books and files, containing notes accumulated over the years, was built out at the back in 1957. A new wrought iron gate incorporating the initials E P is a reminder of and a memorial to Ella Pontefract. The beams in the dining room so laboriously cleaned and polished are still there, but the stone floor because of damp has been replaced by parquet. Other minor alterations chiefly to fireplaces have been made. The kitchen has been modernised and the garden improved. The cottage, we hope, still keeps its character. As Ella Pontefract wrote it rejects unsuitable furniture and ornaments.

It is only natural that after over forty years so many of the craftsmen who undertook the work of restoration and the neighbours and dales people mentioned in the book have gone. But it is still a record of a time when dialect could readily be heard, when old dales people remembered very different times from now, when horses were still the motive power on the farm, when cars, nowadays crowding the village street, were far fewer, and when a more localised way of life prevailed.

M.H., 1984

PART ONE

THE COTTAGE

Mine be a cot beside the hill—S. ROGERS

ALL DAY THE RAIN has beaten on the windows. One minute the fells have been near and lowering, the grass an intensified green against which the wet roads glistened as if for once they had some affinity with the swollen river in the valley; the next a storm sweeping down from the west has shrouded fells and roads, and closed us into a detached world. Each lifting of the mist has revealed the river higher up its banks, and the floods around it broader. The becks, so sluggish a week ago, are rushing torrents browned with peat from the moors. The narrow ditch beside the road, where the dogs lay in the summer heat to feel the cool of the damp ground, is a rushing stream deep enough to drown them now. The hollyhocks that for two months have bloomed in the garden-bed by the house lie prone across the path.

Yet this is not winter. Few trees have lost their leaves or even put on their autumn colouring. The cows are still in the meadows, though huddled like the sheep under the stone walls for shelter. It is autumn heralding winter in a northern dale. The birch-trees bending before the wind in the coppice up the moor road remind one of Greek chorus women moaning of disasters to come; dead, broken branches proclaim that theirs is no undue lamentation.

We have hung our dripping mackintoshes to dry, and shaken off our gum boots. It was splendid out there in the rain hearing the thunder of the becks and the groaning of the trees; but now it is good to shut the storm out with the night. Draw the curtains, pull the chairs up to the fire, pile on another log. Let the wind roar as it will, the strong stone walls of the cottage will protect us. What were those words of the mason as he finished the job? 'There, it's done. And it'll be standing firm a thousand years from now.'

A vain boast? You would not think so if you had seen the walls being built. There is nothing sham about them. Where they look two feet thick they are two feet thick, where they appear to be stone they are stone, not thin facings of it over brick as in much suburban building.

Nor is the notion fantastic. Wars have raged and ceased, but the essential life here has changed little during the centuries. Progress has come so slowly that the community has been able to assimilate it and still keep its stability. In the same fashion the green valley hung between sombre fells, dotted and patterned with stone villages and hamlets, barns and enclosure walls, with the river like a clear thought running through it, has been developed slowly from the waste.

A thousand years from now! The words echo in our minds. If the cottage is to last so long the story of the restoration which made this possible should be worth recording. Perhaps centuries hence an inhabitant may discover a copy of it in a second-hand bookshop or at a local sale, and secure it for what it tells.

Here in this comfortable room, with the howling of the wind, the crackling of the fire, and the smell of wood smoke as happy accompaniments, seems a good time to begin to live again those days of buying and altering the cottage, hard but happy days, with their thrills and disappointments, their worries and un-expected pleasures.

It is not the story of a restoration which moved like clockwork, in which nothing went wrong, and no mistakes were made. We were not very experienced in the type of work which we undertook, and we were dealing with an old building. When disappointments arose the mason reminded us of a local adage whose truth became increasingly obvious as we progressed.

'You know the old saying,' he would remark. '"If you want to do a man a bad turn leave him an old cottage in your will."'

If unexpected setbacks distress you never attempt to 'fettle' one up, for an old cottage, like an old person, has its little ways, and must be humoured. You must be prepared for affairs to run far from smoothly, for anything may happen when you break into ancient walls.

If it is impossible for you to be near at hand and make daily visits, so much the worse, for invariably the crises will come when you are not there. We never approached the scene of operations after a few days' absence without wondering with some trepidation what new complications would have arisen to upset our plans; for awkward angles lost precious inches, and unexpected beams necessitated narrower doorways and at least one window lower than we had designed. Later happenings of this nature agitated us less than the early ones, as experience taught us to modify our first fixed notions.

In altering an existing building, instead of the joy of seeing the foundations neatly laid out, and a house grow cleanly from nothing, there is from beginning to end continuous dirt and seeming confusion. The amount of old mortar and rubble left over from the mere turning of a window into a doorway is astounding. Then one day all the mess disappears miraculously, and leaves a house again.

A great responsibility rests on any one who alters an old building. If you erect an unlovely house your neighbours and the passers-by have to bear its ugliness; but the onus is on you; and future generations may, with a clear conscience, raze it to the ground. But if you destroy or mar an old building you deprive future generations of part of their heritage.

These things considered, there is a unique joy in bringing back to itself and making careful additions to neglected property which has centuries of tradition behind it; in working, as it were, with the past, and creating harmony. The building itself has so much to teach, and there is a grim pleasure in the discipline which it enforces.

Probably the north, and particularly the Pennine region, offers less scope for renovation than the south. The architecture is plain, and relies for beauty on sturdy walls built to resist the weather which comes to the wind-swept valleys. Stone, the native and obviously the right material, by its very nature demands austere treatment. It is a more difficult medium than brick, particularly the small, undressed stone used for cottages. With these the large corner-stones which help to hold the building together cannot safely be disturbed. We had to abandon the idea of a slanting entrance to allow more room at the back door because it was not feasible to cut away the stone.

People accustomed to softer country and architecture are tempted to brighten the walls with flowery window-boxes and painted shutters, but such ornamentation merely cheapens the building, and is obviously wrong because it would not stand the hard weather. A strong wind, even in summer, would rattle the shutters and waft away the flowers in the window-boxes. There are shutters in many of the old houses, but these are interior ones. Good stone sills and lintels are all the exterior decoration that we allowed.

The same applied to the furnishing. As our friends visited the cottage in its various stages some of them chattered of chintz curtains with frilly valances, and coloured china hanging on Welsh dressers; but the cottage itself would have none of these. It demanded something much more severe. It rejected or accepted immediately any furniture which was placed in it, so that there was never any doubt as to whether an article was right or wrong.

As we stood in the garden a few nights after we came finally to live in the dale a curlew wheeled above us for a moment, uttered its burbling cry of contentment, and then spread its wings and turned back to the fells. We were sentimental enough to regard its coming as a welcome when, after a year and a half of war, circumstances made it necessary for us to occupy our cottage under the hills. Its visit also brought freshly home to us how of all birds the curlew best expresses the untamed spirit of this northern country where the fells merge imperceptibly into the narrow valleys. It was going back to its nest on a tuft of wiry grass on the moor, to eggs so perfectly coloured that you almost step on them before you see them. We might take a lesson from it in the blending of our homes with their surroundings.

The chance of the cottage came to us suddenly and un-expectedly. We were not at the time especially looking out for, or wanting one. We were busy that November of 1938 with a book on the whole of Yorkshire, and our minds were spread over its space, concentrating now on one corner of it, now on another, but with no particular emphasis on any. One day as we were passing through the village on our way from the head of the dale we stopped to speak to our friend, Mr. Lodge. The talk turned on houses, and he happened to say that there was a cottage up at Town Head to sell; and half in fun we went to see it. In the past we had explored and fancied cottages in all parts of the dales, but had gone no further. When we turned up the moor road our feelings were not so serious as they had been about many of these; we were merely giving way to the fascination which looking over empty houses has for most people.

The Old Cottage

A few years ago we were taken by two friends, a man and his wife, for a long walk in the Hambleton district of Yorkshire. At intervals through the day they pointed out an old manor house, and said: 'That's where we're going to live'; or a mellowed cottage near a stream, and remarked, possessively: 'That's our house.' All along the way, high ridges with magnificent views and cosy hollows among trees had been chosen as sites for the homes they were going to build. It mattered nothing that the occupied houses had been in the same families for generations and were likely to remain so, that there were no roadways to the high ridges or sources of water near the sheltered corners. They sublimely claimed everything for their perfect home.

It was in such a mood that we started up to see the house, but with the difference that it happened to be in a dale village of which we were particularly fond, and which we were gradually coming to feel was the one place in which we should choose to settle.

The cottage stood at the north end of the village up a road which turns from the main street to run over the moor into the next dale. With its land it occupied the top side of a little green. At right angles to it, and divided from it by a lane, was a cottage facing west and opening straight on to the green. A corner of a third cottage joined this, but turned south away from it. The west and much the longest side of the green was bordered by the road.

In the days before the mullioned windows were replaced by small-paned frame ones, and when the roofs were thatched with ling, this must have been a quaint corner, for all three houses are old. The loftier buildings of to-day depend for their effect on an orderly appearance. They cannot hide neglect; and neglect was written all over the cottage, and spread to its surroundings. The walls, which badly needed pointing, were disfigured at the front by a patch of dirty white plaster; the windows were small and mean-looking; and immediately in front of it, blocking the western sun and the views of the upper dale, was a heap of ruinous outbuildings. It was altogether more humble and ordinary than any of the other cottages we had fancied.

The property was originally a small holding with the house part at the east end. About sixty years ago a lean-to was built on to this end at right angles to it, and this completely shut off the house from a strip of garden beyond it. Near one edge of its sloping roof a thick cushion of houseleek flourished, as it still does. Adjoining the west end, and under the same roof, was a stable; and beyond this, under a lower roof, a privy and a pigsty, the latter surrounded by a small walled yard which opened into a garth.

By the time we had discovered this much, our friend, Mr. Lodge appeared, holding his hands in front of his face and asking if we were going to stone him for suggesting that we might consider such a humble little dwelling. We laughed with him; but I think that even then we had passed the first light-hearted stage and were beginning vaguely to plan.

Presently we found the key and entered, round a wooden hoarding covered with wall-paper, immediately into the living-kitchen. Here there was an undistinguished, fairly modern kitchen range;

but we liked the stone-flagged floor, and, tearing through the layers of wall-paper on the ceiling, we found that the old beams remained untouched. The dairy, a long narrow room with stone shelves, opened out of the kitchen. An outward curve in a corner of the wall showed that there had once been a staircase here, but the stairs, as we first saw them, went up from a small room which was also entered from the kitchen. This had probably been a

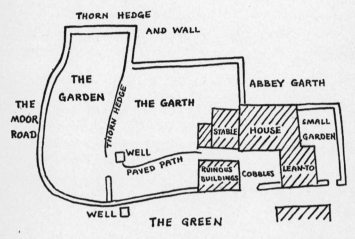

parlour, but the fire-place had been blocked and plastered up, and it had become largely waste space.

The stairs were built up with small stones, and were clumsy and uneven; we found that the village wondered how a coffin could be brought down them. They led straight into the upper story, which had originally been one large room, after the early dale cottage plan. At a later date this had been divided by a wooden partition, but the alteration of the position of the staircase had made it necessary to pass through one bedroom in order to get to the other. The ceilings of both were falling in, and the floors rotting.

There was no entrance from the house to the lean-to, although this was the only place into which water was laid. The water supply was merely a tap at the end of a pipe jutting up from the broken flagged floor; there was no sink or drain. Seeing it as it was then, it was almost inconceivable that a family had lived there until a month earlier.

We examined the heap of ruinous outbuildings, and found amongst them one comparatively whole with a door opening on to the green. This was locked, and we were peeping through the keyhole to see what it was like inside when a figure emerged from the neighbouring cottage, and said: ' That 's ours.'

'Oh!' we said, rather taken aback, for it was at least disconcerting to find someone else's property jutting into what would be one's garden.

The lady explained that it was their coal-place, and had been ever since they came to live there. It transpired that both cottages had at one time been owned by the same person, and, the lower one having no building suitable for a coal-place, the landlord had allotted this to it. When by will the property went to different owners neither troubled to set the matter right, and long usage had made it law.

We discussed the complication together, and presently the owner, having apparently been conferring with his family, came out of his house. We asked him if he would be agreeable to our building him a coal-place somewhere else should we buy the house. After thinking it over for a few minutes, the old man said slowly: 'Well, if ye 'll build me a spot i' my garden wi' t' steeans, Ah 'll gi' thee t' bit o' grund.'

We then explored the garth, and found at the end of the flagged path which ran through it a well. This was built up at the sides and roofed with a large slab of stone, and had a broken-down door in front of it to keep out the leaves and dirt. After branching at the well the paved path continued into the last strip of land, which was divided from the garth by an old thorn hedge. The strip had at times been cultivated, and is always known locally as 'the garden'; but on our first visit it was covered, like the garth, with coarse grass and nettles, tangled together with buttercup roots.

Both garth and garden gave fresh and vivid pictures of the dale at every turn. Immediately across the valley a branch dale joins the main one; and the break in the hills gives a more distant prospect. We saw all this, stretches beyond green meadows of the upper dale, glimpses between buildings of the more wooded lower dale, and scenes of the village street with the hill beyond as background. In almost every view there was some sight of the rampart-like summits of Crag and Wether Fell with the Roman road sweeping boldly over their shoulders.

Scenes of the *Village Street with the Hill beyond as Background*

Returning to the house part we sat on the bink, and rested our backs against the wall of the lean-to. How many brimming cans and pails must have stood for a time on this stone bench before being carried into the kitchen where the milk was heated in a large copper kettle and made into cheese! How many old men must have sat there gossiping as they faced the setting sun, and now and again called out a greeting to a man driving up the hill with a cart laden with coal or produce for the next dale!

Westward, the fells formed a background to a hilly meadow, on the summit of which stood two stone barns. We did not know then what loved landmarks these were to be to us; how the sycamore-tree by the lower barn was to become a symbol of the seasons, stretching its naked branches to the sky through the long winter, softening in outline as the sap rose in the branches, spreading featherlike almost in a night as the buds burst, and slowly settling to the full bloom of maturity.

In the immediate foreground was the little green. We are separated from this now by a low wall and a gate, but at that time the cobbles led straight on to it. Lying as it does out of sight of the main road this cannot strictly be called a village green; many people who profess to know it well would say that the village had no green. It is just a hilly, rather unkempt, piece of common land which has survived.

By the time we rose from the bink we had decided that, unprepared as we were, we would buy the cottage if we could; and we entered that trying period of waiting which seems unavoidable in the buying and selling of property, and endured the uncertainty which followed the inevitable discovery that others wanted it too. This is surely one of the most complicated of bargainings, for the human element enters strongly into it, and personal prejudices and values have to be considered. We have found that people owning houses have certain peculiarities, and we conclude that, now that we have joined them, we have our peculiarities too.

The owner of the cottage, who lived in a village lower down the dale, had inherited it as a child from a relative after whom she had been named. We had several meetings with her, and I remember that we all laughed a great deal at these, probably to hide our anxiety. However, we imagine that, although the lady gave us our few days of uncertainty, she intended from the beginning that we should have the house. During the proceedings the price went up £10, which seems a big rise when it is considered that in 1741 the whole place was sold for £7 5s. It was sold again in 1840 for £62, and though this sum was small compared with our price nearly a century later, the rise was less proportionately.

We eventually took the owner to the solicitor in the nearest market town, and we solemnly put our thumbs on the red seal as a sign of our bargain, and this lost child of a house became ours.

Our deeds told us that we now possessed a tenement or dwelling-house, in 1699 called Coleshouse, but later commonly called Crabtree, with a garth, garden, stable, and other out-buildings, liberty to set up a ladder on the land behind for building, thatching, repairing, or amending the house, and all commonable rights. In the first of the two old indentures which fortunately had been preserved the garth is written 'calgarth', which means calf garth, and turbary is mentioned among our rights. It also expressed the wish that the new owner may 'peaceably and quietly enter into have hold occupy possess and enjoy the said Dwellinghouse Stable Calgarth and premises.'

With our deeds came the realization that as well as a possession we had acquired a liability and a responsibility. This was not a dream house, but stone and mortar, most of which had stood for nearly three hundred years, and which we now had complete power to restore or spoil. For us a great part of the appeal of the little house from the first was that of something neglected to which we could bring back a loved and cared-for appearance.

We resolved that in our 'fettling up' we would keep to the materials and building traditions of the dale, bearing always in mind that the outside mattered as much as the inside, and that our purchase had given us an obligation to the corner in which the house stood and to the whole village. Of necessity something of ourselves would go into it, but we would endeavour that that something should be in harmony with the work of the earlier builders. We and the men who laboured at it should take a pride in it and should enjoy it.

During our preliminary visits to the cottage our neighbours watched us closely as they realized that we were seriously considering it. They were curious and a little apprehensive as to who might join them on the green.   When we had actually bought it they came out separately and welcomed us.

'It 's nice living,' was the general verdict.

A lady from the low end of the green told us she had always called it her house because it was so bright and sunny, and she thought she would like to live there.   She hoped we should be happy in it, and have our heart's desire.

The neighbours in the next cottage told us that it was a warm snug little spot, and asked us in to have some tea.   The old man, Geordie, shook us by the hand, and said: 'We 'll do nothing to harm you, an' if we can do you a good turn we will.'

So we became a part of the green.

An Old Inhabitant

OR THE FIRST FEW DAYS of our ownership we revelled in the joy of possession which had come to us in so swift and unexpected a manner. Our first move was to revert to the original name of Coleshouse. Although we thought with a certain amount of envy of the lovelier names of some of the dale cottages we had admired, it seemed good to revive one three centuries old. It is likely that the name came from a George Cole who for a small part of the seventeenth century owned property in the neighbourhood; or it may be the old spelling of coal, and have some connection with the coal pits once numerous on the summit of the moor. We knew from our deeds that the second name had been Crabtree, but by the time we bought it it had become Rose Cottage on the few occasions when it received a designation at all.

It was obvious that the cottage could not be lived in as it was, and our first inclination was to put it in order as quickly as possible. Believing that the countryman has the right to expect the work in his own place, and that his knowledge of local conditions, weather, wind, nature of the soil, is invaluable, we were anxious to employ only local labour. The 'obedience to custom' which De Quincey admired in the Westmorland builder is still a safe guide.

Our choice of a mason was made some years earlier when we saw a house which he had altered in another village. We never regretted our choice, for he and his son, Jimmy, are true craftsmen of the old type, with a natural feeling for stone, and an innate good taste which has kept them working in the traditional manner where possible. When our neighbour heard who was to do the work he nodded his head in approval, and said: 'Aye, Ah ken 'im. 'E 's aw reet.'

We arranged a day to meet the mason at the cottage. He was waiting when we arrived, his face glowing with pleasure at the prospect of a new job of the kind which he enjoyed.

'You 've got t' finest site i' t' village,' he said. 'I could sell it for you to-morrow.' 'Why,' he went on, as we stood at one end and looked down the property, 'you could build a whole street o' houses on yon land.'

13

That was either an echo of someone else's opinion, or a builder's dream, for we discovered that our mason was, on the whole, conservative.

He drew our attention to the roof. 'You're lucky to have a sound roof,' he said. 'Maks a difference when it comes to repairing. Look at yond 'in,' and he pointed to a waving roof-

The Mason

line which the artist in us admired. 'Aye, maybe it's beautiful to look at, but it means the roof beams are going, and there'll be a big bill for putting 'em right soon.'

Jimmy came up then, and the two went round the building together. Later on that mild November day, as they stood with us in the garth, the older man leaning forward a little after giving an opinion, and looking at us with a twinkle in his eye as if he were quite sure that we should agree with him, and the younger man more serious, seeing through to the finished job as we talked, they seemed to step out of their period, and to symbolize the builders of all eras who have worked and will work in these valleys. Jimmy was later employed on special masonry work on the roads, and the little time he had in the village was spent with the Home Guard, so that, although not building houses, his skill was being used.

At this stage we had no more thought than of repairing the cottage as it stood. The mason considered that £50 would cover the cost apart from the bathroom which we hoped to fit along with a small working kitchen into the lean-to. Local by-laws obliged us to put in a sink and drain and to enlarge the existing windows.

After the discussions with the masons we began to work out our plans; and then came the first set-back. We realized that altering a cottage and writing a book could not be carried on simultaneously, and we put off all idea of beginning the main work for six months. For that period the building stood in its neglected state with the dust accumulating on it as the weeks went by, and a heap of lime which had been brought in readiness on to the cobbles adding to the desolation. The old lady in the neighbouring cottage began to think we had 'rued our bargain.'

We have since been thankful for those months of enforced inaction, and particularly for the occasions they gave us to examine from a fresh standpoint the local building in many districts: the Georgian houses of York, Beverley, and Boston Spa; the mellowed villages of the Cleveland and Hambleton districts; and the architecture of other Pennine dales, each with similar but individual characteristics. We stored ideas ready for the time when we should be able to utilize them, and we began to collect objects which might come in useful, such as the front-door knocker, which we discovered on the door of a house which was being demolished in York. If we 'fettle up' any more buildings we shall endeavour to allow some period for consideration between buying and planning the work.

During this time the men were able to proceed with making a damp-course on the back wall and with building the coal-place for our neighbours, both of which jobs could be undertaken without troubling us. It is doubtful whether the mason would have been able to restrain himself from beginning on the first, for the cure of damp, like the making of drains, is an obsession with him.

''E's a rare 'in for damp is me father,' Jimmy once said; and we can testify that the slight signs of it on our back wall incited his zeal. To eliminate the damp, a ditch a yard wide and as deep as the foundations was dug along the back of the house. A drain was laid at the bottom to take away any water which seeped from the hill, and the house side of it was cemented before the ditch was filled in with stones.

The mason watched the wall carefully through the winter; often he would call on his way to another job and light a fire in the room to help dry out the old damp. Now, after two of the worst winters in living memory, there has been no further sign of it.

Geordie chose a place in the garden for the new coal-place, with which we had little to do except to pay. It was a wet season, and it grew very slowly. In the end the building never became a coal-place. We arrived one day to find the plumber

Geordie Horrabank

laying pipes in the lane which separates the two houses, preparatory to putting a water-closet in one corner of it. Now washing tubs and wood are stored there; and the building which held the earth-closet has become the coal-place. So our neighbour did not come badly out of his bargain.

Geordie was born in an isolated farm-house on the hillside behind the cottage, and lived there all his life until he was seventy years old, when he retired to his cottage on the green. He was so much a part of the farm that he was always given its name instead of a surname; he was known as 'Geordie Horrabank.'

The old man became a kind of mascot to the building. Its progress brought a new interest to a life which has narrowed to this corner. Each fresh step, beginning as a mystery to him, became clear and practical as he watched and considered it. He must have spent most of his day there, apart from the time taken by his daily half-mile walk up the steep moor road to feed his hens.

On our fleeting visits that winter and spring we lit fires and ate picnic lunches among the dust and dirt of the living-room. Sometimes we tore the paper off the walls and beams or scraped paint from the stone mantelpiece. We removed a green coat and a marbled one, and then came to a thick layer of tar. Bit by bit we wore this away by soaking it in caustic soda as soon as we arrived and scrubbing this off before we left. That laborious method proved the most satisfactory one; other suggestions and help made little impression. The mason fancied chiselling it off and leaving the surface rough; but after trying this for an hour or two he decided against it. The marks of his tool remain in a prominent position as a proof of his efforts.

Generally after a few hours we turned our backs on the cottage, and with the dogs took the road or the field path behind us and explored our hinterland. We chose one of the green tracks, old droving roads which are now only used by farm carts and walkers, and whose soft, springy surface combines with the moorland air to make the miles seem easy. The terrier raced up the steep slopes of the pastures which stretched above us to the fells, and sprang over the high walls with ease, while the heavier spaniel stayed on the green road. Once the terrier startled a horse grazing at the top of a long pasture; his white body scarcely seemed to touch the ground as he came bolting down the slope with the horse thundering after him like a monster of the hills. The dog slipped through the gate and lay stretched at our feet panting till he regained his breath after that adventure.

Or we turned right where the road forks at the two barns, and crossed the watersplash, or, if the beck was full, mounted the wooden foot-bridge, and went through an old gate into the gill. Here we walked on a carpet of green herbage patterned with the flowers of celandines and violets to where a sombre waterfall tumbles down the rocks among the trees. We were so glad to find this hidden glen tucked away under the fells that it has always remained just 'the gill' to us. Other ravines must be named to differentiate them; but when we say 'the gill' we mean this one.

The spaniel lay and drank in the pools, and the terrier scrambled so far down the rabbit-holes that only his tail and an occasional muffled bark showed his whereabouts.

At the beginning of June we posted the manuscript of our book, and experienced a sudden bewildering sense of release from

The Gill

work which had governed our lives happily but arduously for over a year.

Now that we could turn with a free mind to the cottage we faced a bigger task than we should have done six months earlier. During that period we had outgrown the idea of merely tidying up the old building, and had gradually come to the decision to extend the stable, and make it into a study on the ground floor with a studio above. We should thus have a working part at one end, while the original cottage at the other end remained as the living part.

We were influenced by the fact that it was not feasible to use the stable for a garage because the approach from the track on the green was too steep. 'It's brantish grund,' Geordie expressed it. The strip of garden at the east end now seemed the best place for the garage. The hilly site meant additional expense in excavation and carting away of the soil, but it was convenient and out of the way.

We never seriously considered moving the cottage into the garth. Apart from the cost, for the sake of a little more privacy and to be directly opposite the good views we should have had a pseudo-old cottage on a building estate site instead of a genuinely old one in the sheltered place chosen by the first builders.

'Aye, it's a snug corner, is this,' our mason said when he came up one evening for the artist to draw his portrait. 'You've only got to walk past on a stormy day to find that out. You're sheltered by t' hill, and t' wind goes right over your head. And that's a consideration when winter comes, isn't it?'

In contemplating which of the periods of the cottage we should accentuate in our alterations, we were at first tempted to go back to the Tudor style. We were attracted to its truly English character, and we admired its lack of stereotyped plan, and the scope its angles and projections, its mullioned windows and decorative chimneys, offered. Also we admit that we rather fancied a studded oak door.

But then, the plain little house had altogether lost its Tudor aspect. The only mullion remaining was one which we found built into the wall. The mullions probably enclosed small three-light windows on the ground floor while the upper story was lit by tiny windows under the thatch. We know something of what these would look like from a cottage a mile or two away, where the old windows remain; the upper ones are little more than peep-holes enclosed by four square stones. So that new mullions, besides having the disadvantage of looking new, would not have resembled the original ones unless we had been content to live in semi-darkness.

Then, too, the Tudor cottage would be much lower, and would be thatched with ling. Apart from the impracticability of putting on a new ling thatch we much preferred the stone roof.

Thatches and mullions being ruled out, it seemed wisest to keep to the small-paned Georgian windows which are now a feature of the village. These were to be sash windows as distinct from the old cottage frame ones, whose only ventilation was a single pane which opened on a hinge. The windows were to be as large as possible, for the walls, being two feet thick, make recesses which, in spite of the wide interior splay, prevent the sun from entering far into the room except when it is exactly opposite the house.

Windows which open by one side sliding alongside the other are used occasionally, but we did not consider these because they appear to be restricting. You cannot open them with the sudden impulse with which you fling wide a sash window, nor do they provide that perfect ventilation which allows the used air to escape through the top while the good enters through the bottom. Casements were rejected because the modern variety are out of keeping, and they have not the same resistance to the weather which comes to this upland country.

In every phase of dale building the severe weather and the high altitude must be considered. The valley runs from west to east, and these, rather than north and south, are the significant directions. A house is described as so far to the west or the east, and our moor roads are the east and the west roads. It is from the west that the driving storms come; and houses facing that direction are exceptions.

The weather is one reason for the prevalent good building. The winter months soon show up bad workmanship or porous stone. Brick is practically useless at this height; it may be used successfully a few miles lower down the valley, but not safely here if damp walls are to be escaped; from an aesthetic point of view a fact for which to be thankful. In this high altitude the variations of the climate are shown in the way in which sugar goes damp and salt turns into liquid if left in an unused room for two or three days.

The front door, in the six-panelled Georgian style and with a simple fanlight, was to open into the waste room now to be our hall. In moving this from the living-kitchen, now our dining-room, we changed the dale cottage plan to one of a house. The stairs were placed immediately opposite the front door, an arrangement not favoured in modern building, but the only possible one in the restricted space of the cottage. They were to branch to a bedroom on one side, and on the other to a

narrow landing which led first to the middle bedroom and then
to the studio, which in a normal household would be a third
bedroom.

The old entrance to the dairy was to be made into a cupboard
under the stairs; and the bathroom was to be taken out of the
other end of the dairy and the waste room. The lean-to was to
become a kitchen with a pantry and a coal-place opening out of
it. From these rough ideas we made our plan.

AS THE ALTERATIONS had become more ambitious we asked an architect to look over our sketch plans to see if they were practicable and to measure up the old cottage and prepare a detailed plan to which the men could work. He arranged for two young architects to meet us there one afternoon, and we suggested that they should first walk through the village to form an idea of its period and style.

We are using the word 'village' throughout the book because it gives an erroneous impression to call it a town, but the local use of the word 'town' is something more than a survival of the Old English 'tun.' It was formerly the most important place in the upper dale, and is still large.

The village in its remote moorland situation was never wholly dominated by one family. The principal owners after feudal times built and lived in a fifteenth-century battlemented hall two miles to the east, but from the middle of the seventeenth century the family were compelled to sell their land gradually during the next hundred years to meet their debts. Part of the property was held by the family who obtained the market charter, and in 1678 built the Old Hall in the village, but this also diminished. By the middle of the eighteenth century the community consisted of several property owners and the tenant farmers under them, some yeomen farmers, and a number of families employed in the various industries which had become centred here— knitters, hand-loom weavers, lead-miners, clock-makers, brewers. It was then a busy thriving place, giving full employment to its own people and those in the hamlets surrounding it, and able to support its village craftsmen in moderate prosperity. Doctors and solicitors found it profitable to settle in it. Even when the market trade was taken by the newer town higher up the valley, this remained a focus for the life of the upper dale.

Now and again it is possible to capture for a moment the sensation of stir and bustle of those days. On rare occasions, approaching it from the fells, we have caught a sudden fleeting resemblance to moorland villages on the outskirts of the West Riding industrial area.

In 1877 the coming of the railway brought a new significance. Goods for Swaledale were delivered at the station; and there was a continual coming and going of carts and wagons over the moor road to fetch them. Swaledale farmers rode over on a Tuesday, and took the train from here to the market town. This movement between the two valleys continued until soon after the end of the last war, when motor transport became general.

Inevitably the development resulted in the steady building of new houses and the rebuilding of old ones, and the village as we know it began to grow. From about 1750 many masons, plasterers, slaters, and glaziers are mentioned in the parish registers. The industrial life influenced the plan, which in general placed tall substantial houses up the main street and smaller ones in squares and alleys opening from it.

The nucleus was the Perpendicular church and the Old Hall, which faced each other across the cobbled market-place. The church, with its sturdy walls and tower, stands as a memorial to past dalesmen who through the centuries enlarged and altered the first aisleless building. Although at the lower end of the village it stands on a ridge, and from the path leading to the south door a sudden panoramic view of the upper dale is revealed. The surprising beauty of the scene presents itself afresh every time we take that walk. It is displayed for the godly and the ungodly alike, for the path is a public footway.

The Old Hall has vanished. Towards the end of its life it became a boarding house, and in 1935 it was destroyed by fire. Its loss is a tragedy which deepens with the years. The four-storied walls, with projecting mullioned windows on either side, had grown old with the village. Itself influenced a little by a slightly earlier hall a mile to the west, it set a standard for all subsequent building. The Georgian houses which followed it are dignified and imposing, and have kept the street line which the

B

The Georgian Houses are Dignified and Imposing

Old Hall established. In their turn they were an inspiration for later builders. There is little obvious Victorian design. The plain walls and sash windows suited the district and climate, and their style was followed well into the present century.

Without the Old Hall to keep that standard alive one fears for the village in the years which follow the war. Those who knew the house can still imagine it in its place, but as the generations pass the tradition of it will fade. The best we can do, if the need for alteration arises, is to keep its immediate successors as a guide, for the eighteenth-century style is yet eminently suitable for the needs of to-day.

The village is notable in that it can definitely be placed as Georgian. Its sister village across the valley was rebuilt much at the same time. Lord Torrington, in his account of his journey in the north in 1792, tells of the work being in process when he visited it; but its architecture is not as pronounced as that of ours, nor is there that strikingly good building which is apparent here, that amount of fine workmanship given scope to display itself.

The large houses have long walled gardens behind them out of sight of the main road, so that there is neither the green of grass nor the brilliance of flowers to brighten the sombre aspect of the storm-weathered stone. Instead, there is the background of fells bringing their promise of space to the grey closed-in street.

This, then, comprised our immediate surroundings, which were to be considered but not slavishly followed, for our moorland road is much more rural in character. The houses, simpler in design, are ranged haphazardly on the hillside, and most have liberal pieces of garden in front of them.

Having seen something of all this, the architects returned from their walk, took out their tapes and rules, and began to measure. They had reckoned that they would be home in good time, but the hours went by and still we saw them poised on the roof, picking their way through nettles, or laboriously measuring the walls by inches. There was nothing uniform about these; not one wall was straight, not one angle as you expected it. We reproduce their scale plan on which we had to work, and the alterations made on the new plan.

The architects suggested a few improvements to our ideas. They made better use of the space allotted to the hall, kitchen, and pantry, and they put three windows instead of two for the dining-room and study. As the work proceeded we deviated from their arrangement a little, but we were grateful for their guidance at the start. Psychologically, as well as actually, the plan proved invaluable as far as the workmen were concerned.

OLD PLAN

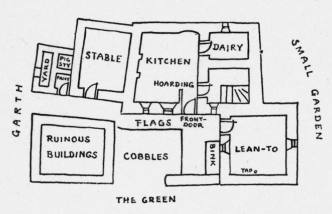

NEW PLAN

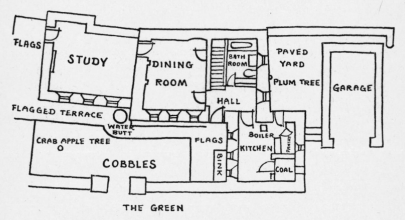

The mason was very proud of it, and of the sketch of the cottage as it would appear. We fancy that it was invariably displayed to the many people who looked in to see how things were progressing. The architects' work ceased with the making of the plans, and we were left in control.

From now on we were never without innumerable papers filled with measurements and plans drawn by the artist for fire-places and cupboards. These were consulted continually on our visits and fingered by dirty hands until the lines almost vanished. By the time this happened it did not matter because we knew them all by heart.

Although we started without a great deal of experience of practical building matters, we felt by the end to have served an apprenticeship to every trade connected with building. Against our inexperience we could set an intimate knowledge of dale architecture, through the many visits we had paid to houses of all kinds in these valleys, and some understanding of the variations and evolution of the plan of early dale houses, through the old buildings and ruins we had explored. We were intensely anxious that the cottage should remain a dale cottage. Mistakes were made on all sides, largely because neither we nor the workmen could always visualize the final result; and some time and money were wasted in correcting these; but there were occasions when, through our mistakes, we achieved better results than we should otherwise have done. We shall not keep back these mistakes any more than our successes, for they may be a warning to others as they were a lesson to us.

We do not declare that to take on the management oneself is an easy way, but it is an enthrallingly interesting one. We became a vital part, necessary to the working of the whole, instead of being merely onlookers making periodical visits to see how the work was proceeding. The result is probably more individual than it would have been under a more cut-and-dried method. Admittedly it is tiring; we did not quickly lose the sense of continuous mental and physical activity. It took us nearly six months of living in the cottage to throw off completely the sensation that we ought to be doing or deciding something every moment.

Nor can we truthfully say that to employ all local labour is the simplest way. The country craftsman is independent, as he has always been, and must be treated with tact. He employs few men, with the result that a fairly large job progresses slowly in comparison with a similar one in a town. He has to think of the future, and cannot afford to refuse smaller jobs which come his way, consequently most of the time during the good weather he or his men will have periods of absence at other work.

Jimmy was in great demand for setting fire-places and altering ovens which refused to draw, or for sweeping chimneys, there being no regular sweep in the village. While working for us the masons received an order to build a wall in the nearest market town, and they were being pressed to proceed quickly with some water-closets which new regulations had enforced in a nearby village. The fact that they might be called suddenly to these hung over us all the time. Occasionally we would dream of the three men departing with their bags of tools to this loveless work, and leaving us roofless and ashamed.

Once or twice on our visits we followed the joiner to remote farm-houses to explain that work was being held up for him, and he would stand a helpless victim between us and the farmer, who both wanted him at the same time. He was also liable to disappear for a few days while he made a coffin. Once, because of three deaths, there was no glimpse of him for a fortnight.

The plumber was a bright young man who left us in a perpetual state of expectation. He kept hens on the intensive system, and these had to be fed before he started out, so that his day always began late and he never seemed to catch up with it. The result was that we never knew when to give him up and either write or wire or even fetch him because the masons were waiting for him. We would work ourselves into a fury against him; but when his smiling face appeared on the green we were so pleased to see him that we forgot to be angry. After an hour or two's work he would run down in the manner of plumbers to fetch something he had forgotten from his workshop, and inevitably he would be snatched away by someone to mend a burst pipe, for most of his work was done in the winter. The plumber lives a few miles away, and it is the custom to waylay him if he is seen in the village and thus avoid the trouble of sending for him. The only time we were sure of keeping him was late at night.

But that is all part of life in the country, where one must take one's turn and never be in a hurry. If there are drawbacks, local workmen carrying on the old tradition can link up old and new as town workmen could not do.

Apart from our comparative ignorance we were at first at a disadvantage owing to the preconceived and fixed notion of the workmen that women understood nothing of building methods. I can best explain the attitude by a conversation which we over-heard between a new man and the plumber. It was on his second day, and he was undecided about the position of the foot which was necessary for the hot towel rail because of the slope of the bath-room floor. He called the plumber.

'Do you think this would be better here or here?' he asked.

The plumber had no definite opinion about it, and he suggested: 'Ask them what they think.'

'Oh, *they* won't know,' the new worker said airily.

Things ran smoothly when it became clear that we were at least happier if we agreed first to any change in the plan.

The mason was virtually at the head of the workmen, and let them know when they were needed; but we arranged with each one separately what he had to do and the cost. We obtained rough estimates from them all; but the mason was reluctant to make a contract for the altering of an old building because of the unforeseen difficulties which might occur. To most of the workmen the idea of giving contracts was like tossing up to decide something, and then not letting the toss make the decision. On our side had the cost worked out at more than the contract we should have felt obliged to make up the difference; for whereas the town builder finishes and is forgotten in the crowd you are liable to meet the countryman whenever you go down the village street. Also on this our first venture new ideas coming to us as the work proceeded caused us to alter the plans occasionally. Where this was done it was done in advance, but it would have complicated a contract. However, with the knowledge and experience we gained, in any future alteration we should force ourselves to keep as close as possible to the original plan, and require a contract before a start was made. Both sides then know where they are, and less time is wasted.

After the six months' delay it was irksome to have to wait again for plans to be passed; but looking back now it seems very little time before all the men were assembled and the work in full swing.

With the mason and Jimmy was their mate, Jim. The two young men, both possessing the same name, almost invariably worked together. Jim, a gay, cheerful young man, always smil-ing, and always ready to help, used to sing in a light baritone voice as he worked. He plays the piano and the drums, and in peace

Loamy presides at a Bench in the Middle

time he and his brothers make up a band which performs for local dances. He has been a soldier now for over a year, and when he was home on leave a few weeks ago he asked if he might bring his young wife to see the house which he had helped to make. He was happy enough in the army, but it was not his ideal life. 'You miss the old spot,' he said, 'and the familiar voices.'

The joiner fitted in his work as it was needed, and was not as regularly on the scene as the masons. Soon another man came to help him. He was good at niggling jobs, particularly at scribing wood into the awkward-shaped walls, and he undertook the fitting of the doors and skirting-boards and the making of odd shelves. He appears often, for he helped us later with bookshelves and furniture. Between ourselves we always call him Loamy.

He is one of those men who are invaluable in a community; besides joinering, he assists at local sales, and he plays the organ at one of the chapels. He is a good singer and a trainer of singers, and has led local choirs to victory at many festivals. His workshop in the upper room of an outbuilding in the yard of his house is reached by stone exterior steps which must be negotiated with care. Loamy presides at a bench in the middle, surrounded, like a wizard, by bits of furniture, carved wood, and odds and ends picked up at sales during many years.

These men, joined from time to time by others, now set to work; and an era of noise and dirt began. The old cottage mutely endured it, and suffered to be made more comely.

Eternity Knocker

*B

The Quarry

A SMALL AMOUNT OF STONE was needed in addition to what was over from the ruined buildings; stone slates for the garage and the extension to the roof, and dressed stone for the new window-sills, the window and door lintels, and the stairs; but this was far from easy to obtain near at hand, for no quarries were working in the upper dale.

When the moor was enclosed in 1819 two quarries were allotted to supply stone free for building the fences. One was in the gill; and after the walls were completed this provided material for a few houses built in the early nineteenth century. Since then trees and grass have covered up all signs of its activity, and one would hesitate to spoil its beauty by opening it out again.

The second, marked on the award as 'Dirty Quarry,' is now the rubbish tip just below the moor, and is always referred to as Dirty Wharrell, 'wharrell' being a dialect word for quarry.

Visitors from the town are apt to look askance at the tips, which make ugly blots in otherwise beautiful landscapes; but they would see them from a different aspect if they had experienced the difficulties of getting rid of ash and unburnable rubbish in the country. It must go somewhere, and without the tips there would be more of those odd corners filled with tins hidden by nettles in summer, but exposed in winter, and more miscellaneous dumps might sprawl on the banks of becks and rivers to be washed down in flood times. We have covered in for ever in our garden a heap of ash which, from its size, might have been started by the first inhabitants.

To this inglorious but necessary end, then, the second of our public quarries has come. Other former sources of stone were two quarries run for profit a few miles higher up the dale. The best stone was obtained from Stagsfell on the north side. It is of a fawnish colour, and, being very hard and wearing smooth and glossy, was in great demand for floors, steps, and hearthstones. A daleswoman, telling of her home as a girl, said that she never minded washing the stairs and floors because they were of Stagsfell stone, which paid for it. But the flags had the defect of being feather-edged; that is, instead of being of an even thickness they tapered off, a drawback which was one cause of the closing of the quarry.

The grey stone from Burtersett, on the south side of the valley, had not the same wearing qualities; it was inclined to shell when used for flags or roofing slates. But this was an important quarry, employing a good number of men in its day, and it supplied stone to places out of the dale. It was used for several houses in the neighbourhood, and it was a suitable material for mantelpieces because, being soft, it stood the heat well. Some of its most pleasant memorials are the paved 'trods' which form short cuts across the meadows and pastures of Upper Wensleydale.

The shortage of local stone has made the farmer value what he has. If a barn goes out of use the slates are taken off and stored for future repairs, and the rest of the stone is used gradually for mending the walls. It is good to see the heaps standing in readiness, for where there is none handy corrugated iron and concrete are apt to be substituted when a repair becomes necessary; but this new value meant that we could not rely on such sources for what we required.

We managed to secure enough slates for the extension to the roof from cottages which were being demolished in the town of Richmond, twenty miles away, but we still needed the rest.

After making inquiries, Jimmy discovered that Hill Top Quarry, at the head of Swaledale, could supply the stone which we required.

This quarry on the windswept moor, situated above the last houses in the dale and in Yorkshire, was first opened to obtain stone for buildings connected with the lead mines: the smelt mills, washing-places, and engine-rooms, whose ruins are dotted over the fells. It was rented from the lord of the manor by a lead mining company; and several men were employed in quarrying and dressing. It also supplied stone for the enclosure walls; the farmers paid threepence a load for this, and carted it away themselves.

When towards the end of the nineteenth century the lead mines began to fail, the father of the present tenant rented the quarry. In his time, several houses in the upper dale were re-built with material from it, but the biggest trade was in roofing slates, hearthstones, and flags. A great quantity was sent over the county border into Westmorland, the west country, as we call it. Farmers from that district remember the time when there were always piles of stone waiting at Hill Top Quarry to be taken into their county.

The son followed his father, and now, an elderly man himself, he works alone because there is not enough trade to allow him to pay a man or boy to help. Even if there were he doubts whether any young man to-day would wish to learn and carry on the industry in this remote place.

'They all want cement nowadays,' the mason once said to us when we were discussing building material. His remark set us thinking on how this has happened. It is not exactly that cement is preferred to stone even now, but it is chosen because it is cheaper, and the mason, who has his living to make, must supply it. Travelling as it does in a dry, concentrated form, it costs much less in transport than heavy and cumbersome stone. That the traditional building material is no longer profitable to work is a result of the same economic system which has killed the country crafts. Perhaps the post-war plans for a fuller and more self-supporting rural life, a life which allows more of its able young men to remain in the country, will restore some of these to us.

The quarryman lives in the last village up the valley, and cycles the three miles to and from his work. He is a spare, alert man with a pleasant network of lines at the corners of his eyes formed by long exposure to wind and weather. In order to obtain the quantity of stone we required in the necessary time the two younger masons turned quarrymen and worked with him for a few days each week. This meant a slowing down in the building, but it proved an advantage in that each piece was picked by them for its particular place, and dressed and numbered at the quarry to avoid unnecessary carriage.

We paid one visit when our men were working there. It was a November day, nearly a year after we had bought the cottage;

The Quarryman

but now the country was at war. For a few hours we had escaped from intensive ambulance-driving instruction and first aid and gas lectures, and it was a consolation to come from their strangeness to find little changed here. There was stillness and peace as we went up the road and through the gate on to the open moor, where ahead and westward the hills of Swaledale appeared, a medley of peaks and rolling summits enfolding one another into infinite distance.

So we came to the signpost on the triangle of grass where the road forks. The post was later removed, but on that November day its guiding hands still gave life to the road, so that passing it you felt to be one with all the travellers who had marked it as a stage on their journey. Then down a deep gully flanked on the east by limestone crags, past old farm-houses on the tossed land, we were in Swaledale. Up through grey villages and hamlets, now beside the river, now leaving it far below, until, above the last farm-houses, we came to where the lane turned over the moor to the quarry. A farmer coming along the track with a low cart filled with slates to repair a barn roof made a picture which one would like to see oftener in this countryside.

The quarry extends over a large stretch of the moor; and paths diverge to the various sections which have been opened out to obtain the different thicknesses of stone. Here and there beside them dry walled huts have been made for shelter and for holding tools. A keen east wind cut our faces as the quarryman led us along the maze-like ways. We came first to where the two men were measuring and dressing the slabs. Both of them had proved clever and interested helpers, and had enthusiastically searched all corners for the perfect material for each purpose.

'That's where the stone over your garage door came from,' the quarryman said. This is a fine slab over nine feet long and beautifully marked. Along another track he showed us where he had hacked the roof-slates from thinner layers. He had taken the lintels and sills from still another section where the strata became thicker again.

It was a new experience to look down on enormous pavements instead of up at tall escarpments which are the familiar idea of quarries. Our chief impression was of the sheer beauty of clean yellow stone. Seeing it thus newly exposed to the light with its water markings clear made it easy to realize the moor as an ocean bed.

The three men working together gave an air of activity and movement which is not typical. As I write I am reminded of a visit with a dalesman this summer to fetch some flags for garden steps. We talked of old days when our local butcher used to ride over the moor into Swaledale in a high open trap to sell meat. Where farm-houses stood far from the road it was his habit to stand up in the trap, cup his hands round his mouth, and shout: 'Mary Ellen, Mary Ellen, do you want owt?' The farmer's wife usually opened the door, shouted back: 'Ah 'se cu'in',' and, after fetching a plate and some money, ran down to the trap in the road.

'Oh, aye,' the quarryman said, 'Ah remember Azariah. Let's see, he used to come down wi' a shandray and a galloway, didn't he?'

A shandray and a galloway! They seemed to belong to another world, to the days when the tradesman's wife used to ride pillion behind her husband. An old lady now, she remembers vividly returning over the moor road when, at the steep bend by Crow Trees Farm, owing to the slant of the horse's back as it took the hill, she overbalanced and slipped over its tail into the roadway.

It was very quiet in the quarry on that second visit. Our friend, working in a far corner on fresh ground, was cutting out stone slabs four or five inches thick. He had reached a small ledge which he had made by first paring off the heather, then removing the rubble, and finally the layers of shale above the flags. As we arrived he had just loosened a large slab, and was shaping it before lowering it to the path. He chipped along it with the chisel where he wanted his edge, raised one end higher than the other on a few stones, gave a sharp knock, and the slab broke exactly as he had intended. He lowered it from the ledge and carried it into place himself, refusing our offers of help, for there is a knack which only experience teaches in handling stone. The man is master of his medium, and calmly and decisively attacks jobs which to the uninitiated seem impossible for a single person. The largest flags he cuts are hearthstones; and he reckons these large if they are eight feet long, though he once cut and moved one nine feet long himself.

When the quarryman first took over the tenancy his accounts were paid annually. He made them out at the beginning of September, to be ready for Muker Show, the one day of the year when he was sure of finding the farmers at home as he journeyed back up the dale. One of his customers was a man named Matty Ned, who was under the thumb of a domineering wife. On one occasion, after paying his account, he eagerly accepted the quarryman's invitation to go to the inn for a pint of beer, but his wife stepped in front of him.

'Tha sall na gan. Tha sall na gan,' she said.

But this was show day, and a special courage came to Matty Ned. 'Thee hod thy noise,' he said. 'Ah tell thee Ah *is* gannin',' and flung open the door.

His courage was short-lived, for, in the quarryman's words, 'He sipped his beer at the inn right quickly, and went back.'

We left the workings for a time, and walked over the moor which is its setting. Nature is on the grand scale here with long sweeps merging into each other in an illimitable expanse which continues over the county border. The slopes and deserted

valleys are covered for the most part with bents and clumps of
rushes whose brown flowers on that day cast a warm tint over
them. Here and there a dark patch of heather showed where
millstone grit was at the surface.

A few weeks before the outbreak of war we were talking about
English country to a Norwegian who knew it well. We stood at
the doorway of his house, looking across a narrow gully from
which the mountains rose almost sheer, their unclothed rocky
peaks silhouetted in stark shapes against the sky.

'I like your English Lake District,' he said, 'but not your
Yorkshire dales. Those sweeping hills frighten me if I stay
long amongst them. I do not understand them.'

We tried to explain to him the opposite reaction of those to whom
these long sweeps are satisfying; that they feel shut in by the steeper
hills of the Lake District and his country, and unable to draw deep
breaths of invigorating air as they can on the broad fells.

The feeling of untrodden places on our hill-tops is often an
illusion. As we stood we heard the tap tap of the quarryman in the
distance; startled sheep below us told that a shepherd and his dog
were passing that way; and westward a peat pot showed where a
farmer had cut fuel for his fires. Away on the slopes of the
lonely valley of Sleddale a patch of green so vivid that it might
have been spilled on the fell marked a meadow wrested from the
moorland. Every summer the farmer whose sheep graze on the
common comes with some members of his family the six miles
from his farm-house and makes hay there.

Far below, where two becks join to become a river, ruined
buildings told of the lead-mining industry carried on for centuries
on the fells; almost at our feet was a covered channel made to carry
water to the washing and smelt mills from a near-by tarn.

Hill Top has a more melancholy air than the tarn on our moor.
Lying on the summit of the fell, with no hills sheltering it, it seems
to express the spirit of loneliness. Curlews and gulls calling out
in anger as you approach, and the lapping of the waves on its
shores, accentuate the silence which broods over it. Yet it too
is frequented by man. Shepherds come searching for sheep
drowned in its water, farmers visit its shores in summer for silver
sand which they use for sharpening scythes in hay-time; others
fetch the sand to mix with cement; and walkers seek it out on the
moor. But they come and go, and the silence remains.

The quarryman, still busy when we returned, seemed a timeless figure, as permanent as the material in which he worked. Yet, unless a younger man rises up to follow him, heather and grass will quickly clothe the stone he has uncovered, and the sound of hewing will be only a ghostly echo.

Our up-and-down route was that which the lorry man took when he went to fetch the stone. He was very occupied at the time, and often it was evening before he set out with the two masons. On those nights they finished loading in the moonlight, and made the journey home with the heavy wagon over the Buttertubs Pass higher up the valley.

The men took the journeys in a spirit of adventure. It was on one of them that they found and rolled down the gully to the lorry the enormous limestone boulders which, in accordance with local custom, crown our gate-posts. We have never seen finer or more shapely specimens than those they brought for us. The wild thyme which was growing on them is still alive, and house-leeks now thrive with it. The masons were anxious to know what we thought of the stones, and Jimmy said to us: 'The general opinion of the village is favourable.'

The new stone fits so well into the cottage that few can tell which is old and which is new. But the quarryman knows. One day, when the alterations were nearly completed, he was given a lift over the pass, and called to see us. As he went round the house he picked out his own stone from the rest, every lintel, sill, and corner-stone, the garage slates, the stairs, the flags in the courtyard, the material for the fire-places. As he noted each piece he was seeing it as it had lain in the quarry, and measuring and cutting it again in his memory. There was mingled pride and satisfaction in his face as he saw that his stone had been well used. He came finally to the long slab above the garage door.

'Aye, it 's a fine piece o' steean, yond,' he said.

Norwegian Farms

IN NORMAL TIMES we should not have deserted the cottage at this stage, but these were not normal times. The shadow over Europe was deepening; even here in the dales we were saying, not 'Will there be war?' but 'When will war come?' It was as if a door were slowly closing to cut us off from the rest of the world; and we felt that we must snatch a long-planned visit to Norway before war shut it peremptorily and for an indefinite period. It was like fitting in what pleasures and opportunities one could before the coming of a hard winter.

Our great interest in Norway lay in its ancient connections with the dales, connections not so strong perhaps as the Lake District can boast, but strong enough for their influence to have survived until the present day. We were familiar with some of the legacies of the Viking settlers in such words as 'fell' and 'beck,' and in our place-names and dialect. We wished now to compare the life of the country from which they came with the present life in our dales. To see how each had deviated from the first common stock promised to be a helpful preparation for residence in a dale village.

As we dared not be away for many weeks lest things went wrong with the building in our absence, we chose to explore one corner well rather than to emulate the tourists 'doing the fjords,' and we picked the Hardanger district for its beauty and accessibility.

We do not claim to be able to write with authority on a large part of Norway from that short visit and an earlier one of the artist's, but we feel that what we saw of the life and people of one corner of it in its relationship to a similar part of England has a place in this book.

We started in the middle of June after two weeks' concentrated work putting everything in order at the cottage. Whilst having tea in Newcastle we wrote four letters giving final instructions; then at the quay we stepped straight out of England into a Norwegian boat with a foreign crew and foreign food.

Perhaps we set out with too strong a feeling of the likeness between that country and ours, because the brightly painted wooden houses dotting the shores of the Bergen Fjord seemed alien and ephemeral after the solid stone ones in which our interest was then centred. It took a little time to adjust ourselves to the fact that the traditional building material here was wood. In the country districts, where the wood was chiefly stained brown, this seemed right and natural, and the farms appeared to grow out of the landscape.

Though the likenesses between the two countries became more apparent the longer we stayed, there were essential differences, such as the use of the waterways for travel and transport. Our dale rivers are features of interest in the valleys, but the fjords govern the mode of life. Larch and fir trees are actually floated down them to their destination. The arrivals and departures of the steamers with their passengers and cargoes including anything from small parcels to cows and goats on their way to the summer pastures are occasions in the day. The strangest cargo we travelled with was a corpse. It was taken aboard, very silently, in the dusk about ten o'clock in a wicker coffin with only a ledge over the head for a lid, and placed in a little cabin near the gangway. It seemed an appropriate last journey for one of this race whose life has always been connected with the water.

There was no resemblance in the grim mountains to our fells, but the smaller valleys had much in common with the dales. Jordal, to which we were first attracted because an early version of our own river name was Jor, stands out particularly in our memory. There was no roadway to the upper part of the valley, but one, tunnelled in parts through the solid rock, was in process of being made at the lower end. The work was done by the farmers after a new custom of the country by which the Government paid for the material if local men undertook the labour. The resulting good roads to remote places enabled produce to be transported easily from the summer *seters*.

The Jordal beck was rocky like our dale becks, and the few farm-houses above it settled into the hillsides as our farm-houses do on similar sites. A few sheep grazed on the mountains, but the chief flocks were goats; one farmer kept a herd of a thousand in the summer. They wander down the mountain sides of their own accord at milking time, and give warning of their coming whilst they are still far up the slopes by the tinkling of the bells hung round their necks.

At the head of the valley we stopped at a house to ask for some coffee; and the mistress invited us to sit inside while she prepared it. It was a more primitive dwelling than any we should find in Yorkshire to-day. As in most Norwegian houses there was an inner porch which provided an entrance and a place for wet coats and boots; a dairy opened out of this; and the rest of the house was composed of one large room which was kitchen, sitting-room, and bedroom combined; there was no upper story. It was heated in the custom of the country by a closed stove. The furniture consisted of a large cupboard, a few chairs, a table for meals, a smaller table on which stood an old-fashioned gramophone with a horn, and a large bed built into a corner of the room, as was once the custom in English country districts. In some earlier renovation to our cottage the side of an ancient bed, pierced with holes through which the rope which supported the straw mattress had been threaded, had been used as a beam.

The Norwegian mother was anxious for her daughter to entertain us by playing a violin which was hanging on the wall, but the girl, who was about eight years old, was too shy. Instead she ground the beans and helped her mother to make the coffee. From a large chest, which acted as a seat to the table, they brought what is called *flatbrød*, which is made with rye or barley flour, and rolled out very thin and baked till crisp; enough to fill the chest is made at one baking. It seemed their equivalent of the haverbread which was once the staple food of the dales. We were also given, as a special delicacy, a saucerful of sour cream which the mother showed us by pantomime should be eaten with sugar sprinkled on it.

Our communication was largely by signs, because the mistress could not understand our halting Norwegian. She told us the names for the various articles on the table; and when we repeated these in our hotel that evening we found that we had been learning a local dialect quite different from the modern language.

The whole atmosphere of the house seemed to belong to an era long past in this country, as did the life in the summer *seters* which we passed on our walk home. These small wooden houses, which are occupied during the summer months while the goats, and in some parts cows and sheep, graze on the mountains, represent a flourishing side of Norwegian country life and the part played by women in it. The women run the *seters* alone while the men remain to work the lowland farms and only come up to them once a week to fetch the cheese for the market; this system of farming takes the fullest advantage of the wealth of the mountain pastures.

We saw two varieties of cheese made, a plain yellow one, and a rich brown one, called *gjetost*. The *gjetost*, which is very popular with the Norwegians, is made by heating and stirring the milk for a considerable time in large copper pans on the wood fires in the *seters*. It has a sweet sharp flavour, and is so rich that a thin slice cut off and held over a lighted match will burn.

We know by names such as Summerlodge in Swaledale and places in Wensleydale with the suffix 'sett' or 'seat,' meaning shieling, that this mode of life was once followed in the dales as it was in the highlands of Scotland, but the custom died out early. Perhaps the inconvenience of the family life being broken up for the summer was a cause; one wonders what a dale farmer to-day would do without the womenfolk to help with the hay.

Farming presented the most interesting comparisons between the two countries. Men who have reclaimed farms from the waste are allowed to occupy them free of charge. The house and barn are built of wood from the forest, and the farm becomes practically self-supporting. Enough potatoes, vegetables, and corn to supply a proportion of its needs are grown in long strips near the house. At that time the system differed completely from dale farming; but the war, enforcing a certain amount of ploughing here, has brought the two nearer. It is to be hoped that the practice of providing for the household from the land will be developed further, and become as popular as it did in Norway once the prejudice against green vegetables, which the people called 'grass,' was overcome.

As in the dales the hay harvest is the principal one; but, whereas here the weather is the absorbing topic when hay-time draws near, and a bad season means that work drags on into the autumn, the Norwegian farmer, sure of getting some wet weather in his hay season, mutely accepts it. The dalesman, knowing that thunderstorms may unsettle the weather, mows one meadow at a time, but the Norwegian cuts a mere patch. If the season is fine the grass is left on the ground to dry, but it is more often hung on wire fences so that the heavy rain rolls off it and it quickly dries again in the wind and the sun. These fences, hung with five or six rows of grass, have the appearance of thick hedges. The method of leading is similar to that of the dales: the hay is carried to the barns on low carts or sledges called *sleder*.

If the mare which pulls the sledge has a young foal she is allowed to have this with her in the hayfield, where it follows her to and from the barn. Foals also run with their mothers on the many quiet roads.

The barns are large wooden buildings on brick or stone bases, near to but seldom actually attached to the house, except in the northern districts, where they are built round a courtyard. They are on much the same principle as the dale barns, the cattle being housed on the ground level, often accompanied by pigs, hens, and a few sheep, and the hay stored on the upper floor; but the entrances have more resemblance to those of Westmorland barns. A sloping roadway leads to the upper floor, whose wide doorway is built out like a dormer window, and this forms a covered way to the entrance on the ground floor. The Norwegian word for barn, *laave*, is reminiscent of our northern dialect word 'lathe,' which is derived from the Old Norse *hlaða*. Also the word *baas* for stall reminded us of the dale word 'buse' for the same object.

The cows are chiefly roan and white with broad white stripes down the middle of their backs. Many of them have brass caps fitted to their long curving horns to prevent them from hurting each other when they are frisky on first being turned out in the spring. Like the goats, they are very tame; and the bulls graze on land crossed by open roads. When we remarked on this to a farmer he said that bulls were kind in Norway.

The orchards were something new to us. Apple, pear, cherry

and plum trees, many of them obviously only recently planted, occupied a good proportion of the land, on which also grass was grown for hay. A notable fact about them was that they lay open to any one who passed along the road in—many cases there was not even a wire fence—yet no one seemed to have the slightest fear that their fruit would be stolen.

It was in the small everyday things that we were struck by familiar sights and sounds; the roadside sign *skule*, spelt as that word is pronounced in the dales; the use of the words *røk* for smoke, *hjem* for home, *fjell* for mountain; the way the people gossiped in groups in the country towns; the sudden appearance of quarries making scars on the sides of the fjords as the limestone quarries do on a few dale hills. On one journey, coming suddenly upon one of these quarries round a bend in the fjord, we seemed to slip from the stillness of the mountains to the activity of an industrial region. Two or three furnaces were burning fiercely; and labourers were crowding on to the quays. The captain of the boat told us that the works were running night and day turning out material for British armaments.

There were still busy centres of the hand-loom weaving industry in the villages, where the noise of the shuttle sounded through open doors. Their continuance was made possible to some extent by the sale to tourists, who can buy hand-woven material in the hotels as well as in the shops. The large hotels have counters for gifts in the entrance halls, but the woven work is also hung round the dining-room walls, where it makes an effective decoration. The weavers are using traditional patterns, many of which incorporate a Viking ship or a raven.

The craft of ironwork is also popular, and in this most of the designs are again traditional. It stimulated our interest in blacksmith-made ironwork for the cottage. A log basket which we bought and carried with us on all our moves stands now by the study fire piled high with wood.

A few pictures come often to our minds with added vividness as we wonder what tragedy may have overtaken the subjects of them. We think of two girls picking cherries from a tree by the side of a fjord, and how we bought some of the ripe red fruit and ate it as we walked back along the leafy road. We see two children trudging hand in hand across a sodden hayfield, dressed appropriately for wet weather, as all the Norwegians are, in oilskin mackintoshes and sou'westers. They stood one a little behind the other for us to take their photographs, and though they seemed shy they must have described us at home, for the next time we went through the village their father came running after us to ask were we the ladies who had taken his children's photographs, and if so would we send him one.

We remember a bus drive from one village to the nearest market town. This was off the tourist route, and the bus was full of Norwegians, many of them fair with the characteristic high cheek-bones and small turned-up noses. Our driver took the winding road following the shore of the fjord as if he were the sole user of it. Round a bend we came suddenly upon two cyclists. One of them managed to reach the grass at the side, but the other was so startled that he fell off his bicycle and lay in the road in front of the bus. The driver pulled up, and stolidly waited for the man to move out of the way. Every one watched the incident, but no one spoke, and in a few minutes we were rushing along again. Suddenly two children at the back of the bus began to giggle. The driver said something which we did not understand, and in a few seconds the whole bus was rocking with laughter. Voices rose and fell in volume as bodies swayed backwards and forwards. Then, as suddenly as it began, the laughter ceased, and solemn faces looked out again at the rain splashing on the road.

There was the lady at the little hotel at Bakke who longed to talk to us, but whose English was no better than our Norwegian. Often we were alone in the dining-room with her. She greeted us with half a dozen quick sentences, then shook her head and wrung her hands in exasperation at our blank looks, and said slowly: 'I cannot spik English.' Then, one by one, she named the objects in the room, and we repeated them after her. This communication became a ritual aided by a waitress who spoke Americanized English.

And there was the farm-house which interested us particularly because it was being renovated. A section from top to bottom had been cut cleanly out of the middle and was being replaced with new wood. It seemed an easy reconstruction when we thought of the work on our stone cottage. That was a day when rain fell unceasingly; not ordinarily heavy rain but torrents which blotted out the landscape so that there seemed nothing in the world but sheets of water joining the water of the fjord.

Even though the likelihood of war had made us take the holiday when we did, it was strange to find Norway more pre-occupied with the thought of it than this country. Inevitably the conversation turned to the threat of it as soon as it was realized that we were English. It was a shock to our pride to discover personally how much Munich had lowered our national prestige. England decadent, England blind, were constantly recurring themes. The people liked the English, but almost against their will they admired the German efficiency, which they said would get the better of us in the end. England had refused to see what was coming, and she would fall to the status of a secondary nation; in fact had already fallen.

We encountered the attitude first on our second day when we shared a car with two ladies for the ten miles from the nearest station to our hotel. They were of the well-educated, rather proud and reserved class, and were at first inclined to be resentful of our presence, although it was a large public car. They chattered excitedly to each other and the driver and ignored us until, hearing us use the right pronunciation for 'ei' in such names as Stalheim and Eide, they warmed towards us. Most English people say 'i' not 'ay,' they told us. Then, as if that were the uppermost thought in their minds, they began talking of the chances of war, and we were surprised to hear one of them say: 'I suppose you 're having a very difficult time in England just now, and you 're all very frightened.'

The captain of a fjord steamer was the next to pity us. Too many old men were leading England to ruin, he said, and she was ignoring her best statesmen, Churchill and Eden. Norway as a spectator had watched the drama, and she knew. Hitler would attack Poland, and still England would not fight. He told us of the German pleasure cruisers which were coming weekly up the fjords packed with German working-class families who brought their own food and enjoyed a cheap holiday. The tourists took photographs of the country and the ports on the fjords, but they never landed. He admired the organization of these cruises, but was blind to the danger they presented to his own land. He had the national independence and arrogance which debarred him from seeing his countrymen's faults. Yes, he said, he knew England; he had called at many of her ports; he thought it was an ugly country, full of slums.

There were the other ladies in the Bakke hotel who spoke in low voices to us as if we were already doomed. And the pleasant man in the Bergen bookshop who informed us that the news was grave that morning; but whatever happened England would choose appeasement again. His was an attractive shop; and we wonder what literature he was allowed to sell in it during the war. Or does it lie in ruins by the quay ?

But if the inevitability of war was clearer to the average Norwegian than it was to the average Englishman, they continually classed themselves as outsiders. Many realized the danger of their ports being bombed; one man we met had rented a *seter* in the mountains to which his family could flee in case of war; but they did not think of themselves as actual participants.

It seemed an augury of the future that, whereas our journey out was still and sunlit, our return was on the worst sea of the year. It was one of those crossings when in the presence of damped table-cloths and a likelihood of being jerked uncontrollably across the room at any moment all dignity goes. We were ordered to bed at eight o'clock, and our last memory is of a talk with the steward who caught us as we were spun round a corner on the way to our cabins. He was a student at Oslo University, and worked as a steward in the vacations.

Midway between his country and ours, with the sea dashing and roaring against the ship, he told us in faultless English of his life in Oslo, of his studies, and his delight in languages. His people have learnt much from ours; but as a young nation they can teach us much of progressive education and the lack of rigid class distinctions, and perhaps help us to regain our national youth. Later, each in our turn having made the choice for freedom, we were joined in purpose as never before.

So with the door still closed against them, we remember those people whom we met so fleetingly, and who yet in the strangeness of fate are wrapped up with the story of the cottage.

Jimmy and Jim

GREAT STRIDES had been made at the cottage in our absence. Piles of wood were stacked in the garth, and sand, lime, and mounds of excavated earth were heaped against the wall. The mason had obtained permission to use a 'shake hole' up the moor road as a tip for the earth and rubbish from the garage site. We should have chosen to keep the top soil for the garden, but as it had already gone we had to reckon its loss as a result of our holiday. Confusion was everywhere, because the men, aiming to get all the outside work done in the good weather, could not stop to complete any part.

The ruined buildings were almost demolished, and much of the stone was already forming the garage walls. It is probably true to say that in the masons' minds the garage stood in the same relation to the cottage as the stone barns do to the farm-house. Manny, who does our carting, and was at one time in a gentleman's service in Lancashire, looks at it from a different angle. He always speaks of it as the coach house, oblivious of the fact that the only horse-drawn vehicle that has been inside it is the cart that he backs in occasionally to fill up our small reserve of coal.

The walls were being built in exactly the same way as those in the old cottage, except that they were roughly twenty inches thick instead of two feet. The method was to set facing-stones on each side, and fill in the space between with rubble. At

49

intervals 'throughs' were laid across the whole width to bind
the two together. There is nothing mechanical about the walling,
especially when done with the small uneven stones used in old
cottage building. The mason's experienced eye picks out from
the pile beside him, so quickly that he hardly appears to consider
what he is taking, the exact sized and shaped stone he needs. The
varying spaces between the stones when filled with mortar give
a rough but pleasing effect to the surface.

The same technique was used for the new west end of the
cottage, in which it is impossible to tell where the original building
ends and the new begins.   Here we continued from the old part
the ridge of jutting stones which marks the line half-way up the
wall where the thatched roof ended, and which now has the effect
of a crude string-course. The generous door and window lintels
also stand out in contrast to the rough face.

The garage and all the new parts of the cottage are complete
examples of our mason's work. It is traditional, but stamped
with his design and character, and recognizable as his.

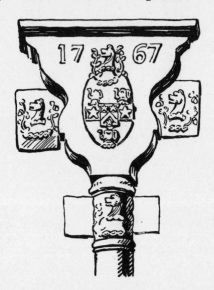

The main street of the village illustrates this individual character
in building in stone. Many of the fine seventeenth-century doorways, with heads carved with dates and the initials of the owners,
are so distinctive that they can be recognized as the work of one

mason. A group of eighteenth-century houses, built of small dressed stone and with shallow carved surrounds to the windows, are good examples of country building. One of these has a relic of the original lead piping decorated with mouldings of elephants and bears.

Four or five houses stand out as the distinctive work of a man named William Dinsdale who flourished about a hundred years ago. His walls are 'watershot' by having the face of each stone dressed on a slant. The process gives them a faintly ridged effect, and the corners seen against the sky appear serrated. His finest example is a handsome house built with broad stones at the base grading to narrow ones at the top, all fitting so well that it has never required pointing. William Dinsdale took a great pride in dressing the stone for his sills and lintels, and often worked a whole day to get a particular one to his liking.

The men put up a simple scaffolding and propped the roof before pulling down the old west wall, and these and the yawning black hole which appeared deprived the building of any suggestion of stability. With the west wall we lost the gable end of the old thatched cottage, the line of which showed plainly, as it still does on Geordie's cottage.

Our second set-back came with the west extension, which was to widen out to a recess at the back to give more breadth to the new end of the room. When the masons dug down they found the foundations of the old back wall higher than those of the front, and they were working from this higher level when we arrived one morning. We could not allow the loss of height which this would have occasioned in both rooms, as we were not willing for the studio to deteriorate into an attic room. Dale houses, being low to begin with, have no extra height to rely on in such an emergency. One result of this is that it is often impossible to underdraw the ground-floor ceilings, which are, as a rule, merely the floor of the bedroom above.

Faced with two alternatives, to raise the roof or underpin the back wall, we chose the latter. The actual work of this was shelved for the time being, but the thought of it haunted our minds through the rest of the alterations.

In spite of worries, this was a pleasant time. It was summer; and we picnicked in the garth, and lazily planned the garden and the decorations. The dogs rolled and played in the long grass,

which could not be scythed because of all the stones lying among it.
We picked gooseberries no bigger than peas from our old lichen-
covered bushes. Sounds of reaping, and the voices of haymakers
came from the meadows. Wether Fell, dim and remote in the
heat, brooded over it all.

Then, as inevitable now as the winter storms, came the outbreak of war to shut tight behind us that door of the outer world.
We had been working against it as much as the weather during
the last few weeks. The west end, still open to the sky, had the
appearance during that first uncertain period of someone's folly.
Our feelings about the cottage became complex. We did not
know whether in its unfinished state it would shelter crowds of
refugees or be trampled by invading armies.

But neither the expected raids nor invasion came, and the
men continued stoically. Fortunately, the bulk of the required
material was ordered and delivered; the few extras which had to
be obtained showed us how difficult building operations would
soon become.

For us life altered in a night. It became a confused programme
of learning to drive ambulances, of attending first aid and anti-
gas lectures, and of helping to sort the scanty A.R.P. equipment
which was all that was allowed us in those early days. We began
to think in terms of tin hats and civilian duty gas masks. We
spent our evenings practising bandaging, and later endured the
weariness of examinations.

Amid these duties the cottage seemed unreal, as if it were something we had known long ago. But now and again we snatched
a few hours here, and some of the horror of the new outlook
slipped away as we journeyed up the dale, and were enfolded in
the quiet unchanging hills. After the first shock, except for the
evacuees, it was often difficult to accept the war as a reality.

The west end was finished by the end of September, and the
whole house was pointed. The pointing, spreading the already
wide strips of mortar to make the wall waterproof, made such a
difference to the appearance that for some time we felt to have
almost lost our stone under it; but now that the building is
settling down, and has been washed by the storms of two winters,
the stone is predominant again.

The interior of the old part was the next work to be taken in
hand. But autumn was drawing on for others besides our-

selves; barn roofs needed patching before the weather broke; shippon floors repairing before the cattle were brought in for the winter; and we who had enforced that six months' break could not grumble when the men occasionally deserted us for these jobs.

Through all the other activities the joiner continued his work steadily and quietly. Except for the hammering we should often not have known he was there. The new floors went down, and the batten doors arrived and were hung.

As the autumn wore on the men overcame the complications of the black-out by covering the windows with sacks and an old rug which we brought up, along with a table and two chairs, when we first bought the cottage. It was somewhere about this time that the mason began to talk hopefully of getting the old part finished so that we could come and stay in it if we liked.

From the beginning the men claimed the living-kitchen, which from now on we shall call the dining-room, for a workshop. It is only just beginning to recover from the indignities thus heaped on it, and to lose the limy cast from the stone floor. In it the mason planned the new chimney for the west end. He built it up in loose stones brought ready cut and dressed from the quarry, and carried these in order to their place at the gable end. The finished chimney was a comely affair, and a source of pride to the mason, who regards it in a proprietary manner whenever he comes up the moor road.

'It's neat, isn't it?' he said when it was finished. 'You'll not see a nicer i' t' dale.'

Our first sight of the stone stairs in place was a momentous occasion. The men were expecting us, and had covered each step carefully with sacking to keep it clean until the last minute. As we opened the front door the mason stepped quickly up the stairs, dexterously picking up each sack as he went, and then stood back to hear our expressions of approval. The spotless yellow steps with their easy rise were an impressive sight, and we expressed our pleasure.

'Aye,' said the mason. 'They're neat, aren't they? Ye'll not finnd better anywhere. There's just one wi' a kind o' a bow on it. Rather lucky only to have one, isn't it? Look at them rises, seven inches all on 'em, and not a bit out. Rather wonderful, that, isn't it?'

After the formal opening we never saw the steps clean again for months; but now continual treading and washing are smoothing the stone, and bringing out its natural cream colour and occasional wavy markings. Left uncarpeted, they gladden our eyes afresh every time the opening of the door floods them with sunlight.

Then Jimmy began work on the dining-room fire-place. Had the kitchen range been one of the old type which are still seen occasionally, with a wide fire-grate hung with 'reckons,' and the oven door and front of the boiler decorated with a moulded pattern, we should have kept it, but it was merely a cheap twentieth-century kitchen range partly falling to pieces. The artist designed and made a scale drawing of the fire-place, and Jimmy worked to this. The stone mantelpiece from which we had so laboriously cleaned the paint and tar was left, and a thick oak shelf was placed on the top of it. The recess, four feet square, was lined with stone, and hobs were built at the sides, with the fire-grate between them, after the style which followed the open hearth in these parts. Owing to the large space between the grate and the flue, a canopy was necessary to draw up the smoke. This, like the grate, was made by the local blacksmith, who at this stage became an important person in the scheme.

A house now stands on the site of the old village smithy which was close to the beck at the bottom of the moor road; but under the blacksmith's tenancy the present one, originally a stable, is beginning to acquire an air of antiquity. It lies at the top of a lane which has the polite name of Silver Street, but is known familiarly as Pudding Lane. This is a narrow alley with houses appearing unexpectedly on either side of it. It is said to have more evacuated children per household than any other part of the village. It also boasts a fried fish and chip shop, a symbol of the importance of the place, which ranks with the market towns in possessing one of its own. The smithy looks over the roofs of the houses up the valley to the overshadowing fells. Often during the day the smith turns for a minute from his work to take in the continually changing beauty of his outlook.

The shop itself is like many another in plan. The horses are shod in a room on the left, where a tang of the stable mingled with that of burnt horn lingers perpetually. Here the stock of iron is stored and horseshoes of all shapes and sizes are displayed. The forge with its enormous bellows, the anvil, and all the fascinating clutter which is the natural furniture of a smithy are in a room on the right.

Blacksmiths, being among the few remaining craftsmen, have had much written about them during recent years, but we do not think that ours would wish to be idealized in any way. He has a lively interest in his craft and in bygone objects which show the good work and taste of his predecessors, but he is also a matter-of-fact and up-to-date man. He comes of a long line of blacksmiths. His great-grandfather, who lived until the boy was thirteen years old, and his grandfather, were smiths in Swaledale.

We cannot imagine the cottage now without the blacksmith's work, as we cannot imagine the village without him to turn to for many needs. Local workmen go to him for gate fasteners, hinges, and snecks, instead of buying cheap machine-made ones. They slip in and order what they want as they are on the point of needing it, and expect the finished article to be ready in an hour or two, which it usually is. He will make a new gate for the garden or grate for the fire, do an intricate welding job on a farm implement, or repair a household pail.

Naturally, the work of shoeing horses still takes precedence. The farmers' intermittent visits during the year resolve into a steady flow as July approaches and horses which have wintered on the high pastures require shoeing for work in the hayfields. The summer visit to the smithy in the lull before the rush of hay-time provides one of the outings of the year. To leave his horse and come back for it in a few hours would be to miss the gossip, tales, and discussion with other waiting farmers to which he has long looked forward.

When we met the farmer from Swaledale there our hay harvest was nearing an end, but his had scarcely begun.

'Ah 've three meadows to mow yet,' he said, 'an' Ah 've yan liggin' abreead, an' yan i' pikes.'

'Ye wern't at funeral on Monday,' remarked the blacksmith.

'Nay, Ah meant to be thar, but t' sun cu' out, an' Ah reckoned Ah could get t' lile meadow led. Ah got it i' rows, an' than went in to me tea, an' when Ah cu'd out it war rainin'.'

'Whya, tha sudn't 'a' had onny tea,' the blacksmith said.

'Neea, but Ah thowt it 'ad faired up, an' when Ah cu'd out it war rainin',' the customer repeated.

We do not wonder at the farmers, for our visits to the blacksmith

c

are never dull and seldom without event. It was on one of the first that he produced from a nail on the wall, where it hung with other rusty articles, what is now our front-door sneck. This is of a design still seen on some of the old houses, a fixed curved

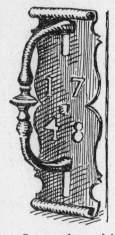

handle with an iron plate which lifts to open the door. Ours has the added interest of having the date 1748 in pierced figures on the plate.

Other treasures have come from the accumulation in the smithy: a poker, an old pair of tongs, a pair of stirrups, some iron fire-bellows which work by turning a handle and have the appearance of a blunderbuss, and a kail pot. This large round iron pan on low feet was used as an oven on an open hearth, where it rested on the fire with red-hot peats piled on the lid. Now it has come into its own again, and stands by the studio fire-place to hold logs and peats.

On another visit he said: 'I found an old fender yesterday. A chap had thrown it out ready for the scrap heap, and I thought of that room of yours, and wondered if you would like it. It's a good one.' He had cleaned the fender, and disclosed it as a handsome article in smooth, solid steel with a pierced leaf-pattern between two narrow bands of brass, brass claw feet, and steel standards fixed to either side for the fire-irons. It is contemporary with our Adam fire-place, and might have been made for the room.

That was the time when, despairing of turning the garth into a lawn this summer, we bought a scythe. We waited while the smith fixed the grass nail, the connecting bar between the handle and the heel of the blade. This is now usually a straight piece of iron, but ours was given a few decorative twists as the custom was long ago.

There is not a room in the cottage which has not some of the blacksmith's work. Each piece is stamped with the mark of a practical craftsman, remembering old things which he has seen and handled during his life in the dale. The round knobs which finish off the curved stays of the dining-room grate are not merely ornaments, but were designed as the old ones were for breaking peats.

The Blacksmith made all the Hinges and Snecks

He made all the hinges and snecks in the house, including butterfly hinges for cupboards, and the handles for the outer doors.   The west or garden door has a twisted ring which can also be used for a knocker.   The back door has loops which are manipulated by pulling upwards from the inside and downwards from the outside.   The garage has again a substantial ring handle, and some handsome hinges.   We are proud of an electric fitting made after the pattern of a tallow dip holder, and of the narrow iron curtain poles with the ends beaten into the shape of spear heads.

The study curtains have headings and slide on small rings across the poles, but in all the other rooms the curtains hang from them by loops of cord.   When the blacksmith was making the poles a customer came into the workshop.

'What 's ta makkin'?' he asked.

'I 'm makkin' t' curtain poles for up at Town Head.'

'Whya,' said the man, 'curtain poles of owd iron!   An' are ye makkin' t' rings to threead 'em on?'

'Nay,' said the smith, 'they 're threading 'em on wi' clothesline.'

The customer laughed uproariously, and thought that we must be having a queer house 'up t' town.'

Our experience with the cottage proved to us the inestimable value of good work.   It is a joy to live with, whereas inferior work becomes increasingly irritating with time.   Surely it is a test of the creative craftsman that as time passes he can look without shame at the labour of his hands.

The Dining-room

THE WEEK after war was declared we went to a West Riding town to choose the bathroom fittings. The arrangement had been made some time, and we kept to it in that strangely altered existence. We paid several visits. The crowds in the streets were as thick as ever, but they were impressively quiet, as if they felt that by treading softly and lowering their voices they might keep away the thing they feared. Theirs was a large city, and they reckoned it would be early in the list of Hitler's targets. We seemed to walk on tiptoe amongst them, ready to race for home should the siren go, for theoretically we were on ambulance duty all the day.

Perhaps the strongest sensation was one of suspension. The essential things, such as eating and drinking and activities directly connected with the war, were being carried on, but others had been arrested like an electrical machine which stops when the switch turns off the current. The plumber's showroom came under this latter category. Unless one was obliged, it seemed useless to think of new fire-places or bathroom fittings in a world in which one's house was liable to crash to the ground any night.

We benefited from this suspension in that every one had ample time to advise us and discuss our problems. Our visits remain among the few bright incidents of those depressing days; and probably they helped to tide over the weeks before affairs became more normal again at the showroom. The discovery on our first visit that Mr. Green had a connection through his mother with Wensleydale made a good basis for our association.

The cottage never having had anything more than a tin bath filled from the boiler at the side of the kitchen range, we were not hampered by period or tradition when we came to consider the bathroom, and we inclined to lavish fittings. We were attracted to a pale biscuit-coloured bath with beautiful solid curves; but Mr. Green dismissed this as an extravagance.

'My dears, my dears,' he said, 'I thought you were buying a bath for a cottage. Do you know how much this one is?'

In the end we chose simple but good white fittings which would not make the passage from ancient to modern too startling. A little colour was introduced by a primrose bath panel and lavatory seat.

One day this summer some friends brought two evacuees, twins of five years old, as a treat to tea. The children discussed the outing as they were going to bed that night.

'And what colour were the cups we had for tea?' the girl asked.

'Yellow,' said the boy.

'Oh, yes,' said the girl, 'just the same as the lavatory seat.'

It was arranged from the beginning that we should have central heating. Besides providing a way of keeping the whole house aired when we were not able to be here, it seemed an excusable extravagance in a high district. The cylinder required a separate section for this, and, the bathroom being on the ground floor, it had also to be lengthways instead of upright. When problems such as these arose cups of tea or coffee arrived as if by magic, and provided interludes in which we came to conclusions.

Plumbers' showrooms, with their rows of unattached bathroom fittings, are often soulless places, but this one, divided into neat compartments attractively set out, was an exception. Indeed, we were tempted to purchase unusual objects, and we were grateful afterwards for the curbing hand of Mr. Green, who knew more than we did how extras, small in themselves, mount up and add tremendously to the final cost of a house.

The fittings arrived before the cottage was ready to receive them, for the work dragged during the early winter months. At last, thinking that it might hurry matters if we took the mason at his word and spent a week in the house, we arranged a visit for the early part of January, by which time the workmen said they would have finished the old part and be working in the new end. They need never come into the house, they said, but could get into the studio just as easily by the windows; a theory which did not work out in practice. They never broke the habit of slipping in at the front door and up the stairs to the studio, through the dining-room to the study, or into the kitchen to fetch water.

The interior walls had to be almost entirely replastered because the old plaster peeled off with the paper or crumbled away when touched. In the few places where the old was good enough to be left, small yellowish-brown stains, caused by grease from ancient cow hairs, came persistently through the distemper, until we finally painted the spots with water-glass, which so far has prevented the grease from penetrating.

By dispensing with ceilings in the upper story we obtained loftier rooms and again were able to disclose the beams. The work on the roofs was long and intricate, because, in order to ensure against wet or snow coming through, the joinings of the roof slates were cemented before the spaces between the beams were lathed and plastered.

The masons kept fires in the newly plastered rooms, and the walls were dry when we came on our visit. Although no more cleaning than a good sweep down could be attempted, the house looked very cheerful with large fires burning when we arrived. Everything was as had been promised until we opened the kitchen door. Here was a scene of desolation, with tools, pipes, and rubbish cleared from the rest of the house filling the floor space. The pure white sink stood proudly in position amongst it like a swan in a dirty hen run, but the beautiful Ideal boiler, with its green mottled finish, failed to rise above the general mess. Forlorn and unattached, it looked as though it would never be a working object to heat our baths and warm our rooms.

But the kitchen was tidy compared with the bathroom, where

the confusion was accentuated by masses of pipes of all sizes, which looked as if no skill on earth could ever disentangle them. In the midst of the litter stood our new bath, unfixed, and with no protection but an old sack laid in the bottom. Its presence there was part of a vicious circle. Owing to the lengthways cylinder there was only room for a very narrow door. The bath would not go through this door, and so it had to be brought into the bathroom before the dividing wall was built. We hope it will last for ever, because we see no way of getting it out or bringing in a new one. It served then as a vague promise that some day this might be a place in which we washed.

The plumber had failed us, and had also prevented the masons from completing their work. We had to resign ourselves to a cold-water tap and a fireless kitchen for our first stay in that hard winter of early 1940.

On the third day the water froze, and the one available tap became useless. Not knowing when the well had been cleaned, we dared not risk using that, and we had to fetch our drinking water from the neighbouring cottage. For three mornings we turned the tap hopefully, but with no result. We were not alone in our affliction. Half the houses in the village had no water, and the inhabitants seemed to accept it as a natural winter happening. Whether or not your water was frozen was the question of the day. On the third morning Geordie shuffled up to the door, put his head inside, and asked: ''As t' watter cu'd yet?' We shook our heads; but an hour later the first welcome drop appeared. After a similar experience the following year we had the supply pipe brought much further under the foundations, and this has proved effective in preventing freezing.

But our chief remembrance of that visit is of dirt. We crunched it under foot, we breathed it, we ate it. Our bedroom furniture consisted of two camp-beds, a strip of old carpet, and a large cardboard box with 'Love to Grandfather' printed on it, a relic of a family Christmas present. Although the carpet was shaken two or three times a day, it always felt gritty when we stepped out on to it in the morning. Downstairs we had the table, the two chairs which had been brought up over a year before and which had been used as sawing benches and plank props by the men, and two camp-chairs. The rest of our equipment consisted of a few odd cups and plates, some large horn-handled knives and forks which a relative had given us, and some spoons from Woolworth's. Visitors of all kinds drank from the saucerless cups, and reclined in the camp chairs as if they were the most luxurious pieces of furniture.

Next to the dirt was the lack of privacy. Camping in a tent was seclusion compared with this. The men were everywhere; from all directions they verged in upon us in the dining-room, which they were still inclined to use as a workshop if we left it for many minutes; they collided with us on the stairs; they met us at the kitchen sink. This scarcely troubled us, because we were busy all the time seeing first one and then the other, and checking up with our lists of measurements. And, the day's work over, it was cosy round the fire at night, and restful to feel folded in the peace and quiet of the hills.

It is probable that the plumber did not believe us when we said we were coming, because once we arrived he set to work in earnest. It is only fair to him to say that the frost had made extra demands on him, and frozen taps and burst pipes were still needing him. He continued to arrive late, and to be lost for hours whenever he went to fetch anything from the village; but, as a rule, he returned, and worked overtime. His mate had been called up, and he could only occasionally obtain the help of an older man from lower down the valley; consequently he was often alone; and a plumber alone is under a handicap. During that week we almost turned into plumber's assistants ourselves. The artist made the better one. After a time I felt that I would rather freeze without central heating and resort to the tin bath for ever than hold pipes and help to fix levels on the uneven walls and floors any longer.

The climax came when one night the plumber said that he could not fit the pedestal to the wash-basin because the broad radiator pipe would not allow it to go near enough to the wall. For half an hour the three of us struggled with that pedestal, loath to let it go, but at last we had to consent to have enamel brackets instead of the pedestal. Gradually the problems were overcome and order began to reign.

Owing to the lack of underdrawing and cavity walls the radiator pipes could not be hidden except in very few places. At first the iron pipes made us think of old-fashioned church heating; but now that they are coloured like the walls they are scarcely

*c

noticeable, and they help to heat the rooms in addition to the radiators.

The plumber's work in the bathroom and kitchen was finished and the dining-room radiator put in working order on the morning we left.   A fire was lit in the boiler, and we just had time to see the steaming water and feel the heat of the radiator.   Upsets were forgotten as we saw the system working well.   Geordie came in and marvelled, and, putting his hand on the radiator, said: 'Thar 's nowt like it i' Toon 'Ead.'

From now on we made regular visits, but always after that first one we arranged to have the floors washed, so that at least we started clean.   We had proper beds for the second visit, and every time we added a little more comfort.

On each stay we undertook one large job of the many we had planned to do ourselves; of them all the most uncomfortable was cleaning the beams.   These are ash, for there are few oak-trees in this part of the dale; they are roughly shaped and trimmed with an adze, and in places still retain the bark.   Fortunately, they had not been painted or darkened with stain, and it was the dirt which had sifted through the floor for centuries and mixed with the paste with which the paper had been stuck on to them which had to be removed.

After sand-papering them roughly we scrubbed them, a wet, miserable job, for the dirty water ran down our sleeves and in very little time soaked the old mackintoshes we wore.   By the time we finished the last beam the floor was a muddy lake which we swilled into the hall and out through the front door as the clock struck midnight.

The following day we told Geordie's wife how we had spent our evening, and she showed appropriate astonishment, and then said compassionately: 'And you coming from good homes, too!'

Later we sand-papered the beams again before polishing them with beeswax and turpentine until they glowed in the firelight.

At this time the green went from bad to worse.   The ruts and mud deepened.   Day after day an enormous pile of marl and rubble lay half-way across the track waiting for the lorry man to cart it away.   One day we took the car out to go and see the joiner, and coming back, in avoiding the heap, we skidded on to the soft grass.   All the men had gone home, and we had to extricate our-

Electricity was made in a Corn Mill

selves in the dark. If we attempted to move, the car merely slid further down the slope, and threatened at any moment to overturn on to Geordie's cottage. We threw ash and gravel in front of the wheels, but it took an hour of constant effort to get on to the track again.

On our third visit we began painting the old part with priming coats which were to last the first year. Mrs. Sharples now became a central figure in the scene. She aired the beds before we arrived, lit the fires, and finally undertook to do the distempering for us. She seemed tireless as she brushed coat after coat on to the new walls. We think of her chiefly at that time as poised on a plank between two pairs of steps while she distempered between the beams. It was another year before the three of us completed the decorations when we came permanently to the cottage.

The electric light was installed in sections as the men were ready for it.

'And you'll have oil lamps,' people used to say when we mentioned the cottage. And we replied, nonchalantly: 'No, electricity.'

Electricity was introduced here about forty years ago by a private company still owned by the family who formed it. It was made in a corn mill whose water-wheel supplied the power. Though it is now a more ambitious undertaking, with a plant further up the gill, it still draws its main power from the beck and a waterfall. Its cost, being higher than a townsman expects to pay for his electricity, debars it from supplying heat for cookers and radiators, but we are glad to have it for other uses.

Its power varies; there is always an element of uncertainty in making the breakfast toast. Sometimes during the evening the light slowly fades, leaves us in blackness for a few seconds, and flickers on again. This happened rather appropriately a few weeks ago when a friend was describing some ghosts of the district. We were hearing about a little man wearing a green coat and peaked cap who haunts the spot on which an abbey stood for a few years until the bleakness of the climate and the roughness of the people drove the monks to a more congenial site. The room grew gradually darker as the teller proceeded, absorbed in his story.

'He comes round a corner of the house and along a narrow passage, and then disappears through a gate. People who have seen him say——' At this point he looked up and saw us as dim shapes across the room.

'Is there anything wrong with the light?' he asked: and the tension broke as we laughed and the bulb slowly brightened.

But these are odd occasions; on the whole the electricity serves us well. There is, too, a satisfactory feeling about the way in which the natural elements of the countryside have been used to ease the life of the people. There is not here the continual force which is supplied by the becks of mountainous countries, where electricity is so cheap that lights in the hotels are left on all day. But the power of the water, a power which can only be obtained in hill country, is utilized for the good of the community.

The finished Cottage

⁶'Now you're heughed,' Geordie's wife said to us after our first stay at the cottage. Certainly we were like the sheep which know their own pasture, but the way was not yet smooth. The stable end had still to become a real part of the house.

The studio was taken in hand first. Probably of all the work in the cottage Jimmy most enjoyed that on the fire-place in this room. Projecting a foot from the wall, it is built up of small dressed stones with a hood of roofing flags, and has a stone bench attached to each side. The fire opening is topped by an arch with a centre keystone. When Jim came to see us during his leave he sat for a long time looking at the studio fire-place, and then he said to his wife: 'I was jus⌃ thinking of the hours it took us to get that arch perfectly even.'

There are four windows in this room: a large one on the south and a smaller one on the west have fine views which seem to catch the hills and the dip between them at their loveliest; a north window and a skylight above it light the recess in which the artist works. Further along the north side a cupboard has been made in place of the old forking-hole through which the hay was piled into the hay-mow. After some deliberation we filled in the putlock holes into which the scaffolding for the original building was fixed and which it was the custom to leave open in the interior wall.

We had a foolish adventure with the roof, on which, as in the bedrooms, we dispensed with underdrawing. This left us with the original adzed beams at the old end and plain planks at the new, a combination which we found unsatisfactory. Had the war not broken out just when it did we should probably have endeavoured to secure beams for the extension to match the old ones; but in the rush of those first few weeks there was neither time nor interest for such matters. The joiner did not know of any, and disliked the idea of them.

It was perhaps unfortunate that a little later several pine-trees were cut down in the artist's home garden, for we conceived the idea of having some of the trunks split into three and using them to face the three visible sides of the planks. They joined together well, and when the plastering was done between them, unless they were examined closely, looked like genuine beams, although for beauty they were rather too evenly circular. But, probably because we knew they were pseudo and not of any use in the structure, we never liked them. It was the plain insignificant planks underneath which were supporting the roof. The artist would disappear into the studio, and, after studying them for a time, would reappear with an unhappy face.

At last we questioned Loamy as to the feasibility of removing them. He expressed himself willing to try, and promised to come up that evening and bring the blacksmith to help him. On their way they called at the mason's to receive his sanction for what they were doing. They told us that they dared not repeat to us what he said; by the next morning when he came to touch up any bits of plaster which had fallen his indignation had abated a little.

The whole proceeding took about two hours, during which time we stayed downstairs and felt like members of a family sitting in a waiting-room while another member has a serious operation. Sounds of hammering and rending wood were interposed with heavy thuds. Dragging noises indicated that one beam was denuded and preparations being made for the next. At ten o'clock the men departed with bundles of wood for kindling under their arms. We crept into the studio, and felt an inexpressible relief. The overpowering sensation had gone and left one of space and freedom. We had banished the fake.

Since then we have painted the planks as near as possible to the colour of the old beams, and we intend to decorate them in a medieval pattern in reds and greens and blues. The wood was not wasted; Loamy had it cut into small lengths at the sawmill, and used some of it to make our front gate.

But that is going forward. At present the men are closing the door of the studio behind them and beginning on the study, which, with its open windows and doorway and the heap of earth rising half-way to the ceiling in the centre, was reminiscent of an ancient ruin in process of being excavated.

The underpinning could not be put off any longer. The masons had a little practice on the east wall in removing one of the enormous boulders which in old cottages were used as foundation stones. It projected for about a foot out of the wall and above the floor level, a position which, though allowable and perhaps convenient in a stable, was impossible in a house room. It was removed safely, but it caused a slight crack to appear in the plaster of the dining-room.

The underpinning on the north side took two days. Foot by foot the men moved skilfully along the length of the wall. They loosened a stone, wedged in an iron girder for support, and, after removing the stone, built up to the girder from the new and lower level. We all joked about it; but worried lines disappeared from several faces when the crisis was passed safely.

Then came the removal of the pile of earth. We still question the wisdom of not moving this before the west end was built up; but the men said it was easier to take it up planks through the middle window and across to the wall, from where it could be loaded on to the lorry. The middle window suffered in the process. The sill and ledges took on a worn, tired look which is still traceable through coats of paint.

A drain was then laid across the floor to carry away any surface water under the foundations, and a layer of cement was put down. This had to be done whilst there was still some slight danger of frost. A picture of the room at the time stands out in our memory as illustrating the peculiar tendency of the men to appropriate anything in the house to their own use. As we were beginning to accumulate a number of things in the old and finished half this had awkward repercussions. One of the articles we had brought was a Valor Perfection oil cooking-stove which we treasured particularly because, besides having had to pay a pound more for it than we should have done a few months earlier, we had had great trouble in obtaining it at all. On this day we came up to find the stove standing on the cement in the middle of the study with both lights blazing. Sand, mortar, and dust lay so thick on it that it seemed a grey instead of a delicate green one. The difficulty was that we could scarcely object because we were as anxious as the men lest the cement should be cracked by frost.

All this time the west door, which was to be half panelled, half paned glass, did not arrive; and one of the old doors was wedged into the opening. At night we heard it knocking against the doorway in the wind like the ghost of a past inhabitant imploring to be let in.

The study, with its three large windows, was to be wholly in the Georgian style. After some searching we found in a shop in York an Adam fire-place which had come from a house in the Shambles, and a pine mantelpiece which had been in Aston Hall, Derbyshire. Continual rubbing to remove the paint with which the pine had been covered had produced a lovely velvety sheen on the wood.

In order to provide adequate height for both new rooms the original plan had given a level entrance from the landing to the studio, and a step down into the study. As the work progressed we found that dispensing with a ceiling in the studio, thus making the room lofty at its highest point, would enable us to raise slightly the height of this floor. This meant that there was a step up to the studio, and that the study was on the same level as the dining-room from which it opened, altogether a much better arrangement.

In our joy at discarding the step none of us remembered that the fire-place recess had been made the correct size for an Adam grate, which requires a much larger opening than does a modern fire-place. When the grate came to be fitted it would not go into the shortened space. It was impossible to raise this, because the top of it was an iron girder which helped to support the wall, and we had to resign ourselves to shortening the iron plates by four inches. That was one of the moments when we agreed with the mason's adage. We were never so glad to see an object finally fixed in position as we were to see that fire-place.

In order to keep the room in harmony with the rather cruder aspect of the rest of the house we introduced a stone hearth and

The Study was in the Georgian Style

a strip of stone between the fire-grate and the mantelpiece instead of the usual marble. To remind us of the room's humble origin, we retained in the wall the iron hook to which the horse had been tied in the stable.

The staining of the study floor was one of those domestic feats which are more amusing in retrospect than in actual happening. We began it in the morning of a day on which we were expecting some of our first invited guests to tea, and we were anxious for everything to look as finished as possible. We used a mixture of mahogany and oak crystals so as to achieve a colour which would blend with the pine mantelpiece and mahogany furniture. Choosing the least conspicuous corner for testing, we stained a small patch, which dried a bright reddish tone. Hastily we put more oak into the stain and tried again, with the result that it was too brown. So we fluctuated, putting now a little oak, now a little mahogany, until the amount of stain we had mixed would have covered all the floors of a substantial house. The difficulty lay in the tendency of a colour which looked brown when wet to dry red, and vice versa. Time crept on, and, except for the testing corner, the boards stretched bare before our eyes. When the last mahogany crystals had been added we finished the floor. This attempt resulted in a brown effect when seen from the dining-room, and a red effect from the garden door; but continual polishing has now blended the stain into a shade which seems to draw the pine and mahogany together. The polishing was finished and the rugs were flung down an hour before the visitors arrived. This was a decorous tea party, and the fevered preparations were not mentioned, but the thought of them accentuated the calm which had come so suddenly to the room.

It is a test of the restful atmosphere of the study that, as I write, a year and a half later, of the trials which went to its making, they seem like happenings of long ago, from which time has taken the sharpness and left only the humorous remembrance. The room has overcome them.

In the week before Easter the masons were busy outside laying the pavements and extra cobbles round the house, making steps into the garden, and straightening out the heaps of earth which had been carted there. In their trade, in which work is often delayed by bad weather, they take little notice of holidays, and they were putting the final touches and mending one of the dry walls when we arrived on the Easter Monday. Then suddenly there was nothing more to be done, and we shook hands and said good-bye, and were left with the completed house.

As the men disappeared over the green, Geordie came out of his cottage. 'Well,' he said, 'ye 've mensed Toon 'Ead up wonderful.'

THERE WAS NEVER A DAY when a large van arrived,
unloaded the whole of our furniture, and went away empty. We
had a small removal when the cottage was finished, a larger one
when we came permanently; packages arrived by train; and invariably on our visits we brought a car loaded to full capacity and
occasionally overflowing into a trailer.

We know an antique dealer who a few years ago removed his
whole stock-in-trade and his household goods with his car, and is
now beginning the same process again, although his wartime car
is an Austin Seven. He also transports his purchases at sales
in this way. Last week, stopping to watch what looked like a
heap of furniture moving up the street, we discovered that it was
the equipage of the antique dealer and his wife, who were sitting
comfortably inside the car with furniture fastened all round it
and two grandfather clocks lying side by side on the roof. Ropes
of various sizes and colours, eked out in one place by a dog lead,
crossed and recrossed over this array. It travelled slowly up the
street, a miracle of packing and a practical demonstration of
what can be done by determination and ingenuity.

Probably we should have been wiser to emulate this system in
our removals. Instead we filled the interior with boxes and
packages, and then somehow managed to wedge ourselves and the
two dogs in among them. The spaniel curled up obediently in
a corner on the floor, but the terrier insisted on perching on the
highest object, which often happened to be a loose hat or a
favourite plant.

The final removal followed the winding up of our ambulance
work in our home town. We had been ambulance drivers since

the beginning of the war, and when at the time of the invasion of
Norway we were asked to take the place of two men as officers
of the depot we agreed. It was a voluntary job, but an arduous
one if it was to be done well, particularly at the beginning when we
were acquiring new premises and putting the depot into good running order. The work, the many exercises and meetings connected
with it, and the cold weary hours of waiting between the Alert
and the All Clear filled a large portion of our lives for this period
They were a constant background to our thought of the cottage,
and by limiting our visits to it were a cause of some of the
complications which arose. It was a wrench to leave the depot,
and the happy party which had gathered round it, but our work
was now to lie in another sphere.

Even after the last load of furniture went, more things accumulated, and these we gathered into a trailer. Innumerable small
articles made an unwieldy load, but we packed them in and
covered them with a mackintosh sheet which we roped as we
thought securely. It was our custom to examine the trailer
load after a few miles to see how it was travelling; but, being
exhausted with final business and packing, once we started,
hours later than we had planned, we relaxed and forgot our
appendage.

A few miles beyond the town of Ripon there was a slithering
noise behind us, and I said to the artist: 'Is there something
slipping in the trailer? We'd better stop.'

As we slowed down a motor-cycle passed and drew in front of
us with two soldiers on it waving their arms up and down violently.
They came up to us as we stepped out of the car.

'Your trailer's dropping things,' they called. 'We've passed
them for three or four miles on the road.'

We looked back on a scene of devastation. The top of the load
had slid forward on to the luggage grid, the mackintosh sheet was
wound round the wheels and trailing in the dust, and the road
as far as we could see was carpeted with books, parcels, and torn
pages of the *Studio*. We gathered up the nearest, and were
considering unbolting the trailer and going back for the rest
when a car drew up.

'Are these yours?' the occupants asked, and handed out a
pile of books and papers.

As they moved away another car stopped. 'This yours?' a

voice said. 'We picked it up a mile back,' and the driver pulled forward a large parcel composed of all our curtains.

Another car brought a bundle of miscellaneous books; and, its two occupants declaring emphatically that they had looked well as they came along and were sure nothing more was left on the road, with the help of the two cheerful young Royal Engineers we gathered up the debris, tied the dilapidated bundles on tightly, and finished the journey. We found then that nothing was missing, and, except for the mackintosh sheet, which was torn into ribbons, the damaged *Studios* and one or two books rubbed at the corners were the only casualties.

The removals were complicated by the narrowness of the door into the studio, caused again by the appearance of an unexpected beam. When anything large had to go in here it was necessary to take out one of the sash windows, and let the furniture in by means of a ladder.

So, in 1941, two and a half years after we bought the cottage, we settled in it as permanent residents. All the rooms now had books and furniture stacked in the middle of them to be out of the way of the decorating. For two weeks paint became our horizon. We moved amongst it, breathed it, and went about smeared with it. Paint tins of all sizes mingled with casks of distemper and pails full of the snowy mixture; bottles of turpentine and linseed oil jostled with pots from which brushes protruded like thick quills on a porcupine. We had vowed to do the work ourselves, partly from war economy and partly because we enjoy painting; and although there were times when, as we finished one room and moved to the next, we felt to be acting like machines, it was a joy to see the clean white coats coming on to the wood under our hands, and to sense the finished appearance of the rooms. Mrs. Sharples preceded us with the distemper, and at times helped with the paint.

The dogs detested it. They could not understand why they were continually being shooed away from the door surrounds and skirting boards. We would see daubs of paint on them, and know that somewhere brown and white dog hairs were clinging to wet paint.

When several window frames and sills were wet together, evening created black-out problems. One night we went to bed in the dark, the next groped through the dining-room on our way to the study. Then Mrs. Sharples had the idea of hanging the black curtains outside by shutting them into the tops of the windows. This worked well, although we were never quite comfortable about it because it was impossible to tell from inside whether or not the curtains had lost hold. One night, feeling uneasy about a kitchen window, we went out to look, and were aghast to find that a corner had slipped. We mentioned it to a neighbour the next morning.

'Yes,' she said, 'I happened to look out, and I saw it. I once thought of coming to tell you, but I was feeling a bit tired, and I didn't bother.' That was in a period of slackness. Since then bombs have fallen too uncomfortably near us to be pleasant, and we have all become much more particular.

Mr. Lodge.

There was little time between painting to put the completed rooms in order. Visitors perched among the mess, and talked to our dishevelled persons. A lady who had evacuated herself here came to call, and seemed to enjoy her tea sitting on a chair barricaded by books. Mr. Lodge came often, and on each visit was surprised to find us still upset.

A family from Harrogate arrived unexpectedly on their way to somewhere else. That afternoon we had considered throwing down tools and having a holiday; and then we had looked in the kitchen and begun on its walls, and so they found us.

Things repeatedly turned out like that. There was the time when we had nothing in the house for tea but a few ordinary biscuits. We kept saying that one of us must go down to the village for the bread and cakes, but instead we continued sewing the clothes-line on to the curtains because we wanted to see what they looked like hung. And then the vicar and his wife called, and all we had to offer them was the biscuits. Probably no one at that time realized how often in those scanty visits we had to make a choice between cake and curtains, pudding and paint.

The priming coats of paint and distemper were ivory; but,

feeling that this had a suburban effect, we changed the final coats to white as being more cottage-like and harmonizing better with the old beams, the stone-flagged floors, and the ironwork. We rejected whitewash because of its tendency to rub off when touched, but had to search to find a water paint which

was not too dazzlingly white. One of Hall's distempers came nearest to what we wanted.

We intended to paint the doors like the rest, thinking that if stained they would look poor against the beams and the oak furniture which we hoped to have. After putting on the first thin priming coat we again played with the idea of staining, and

The original Bedroom Fire-place

the artist experimented on one. She put the oak stain over the priming and worked it in with a brush and a cloth, shading and streaking it as she thought fit. The result was a success, and eventually she did most of the entrance and cupboard doors in this way. Numbers of our visitors have remarked: 'I love your oak doors,' and often I am afraid we have just let them think they were oak. The whole effect was in the nature of a freak, because we should never have reached it without the priming coat which, by filling in the graining, gave substance and also a grey undertone to the stain. The result showed to advantage on the doors of the wardrobe and cupboards which are fitted in over the slant of the stairs in the small bedroom.

The study is the only room in which we deviated from white. Being Georgian in style it demanded cream paint and pale Adam green on the walls. We kept to white for the kitchen, but introduced primrose paintwork. The combination makes a clean, cool-looking background for the green boiler and cooking stove. The exterior paint was already cream, but that too will become white when it is redone, except for the doors, gate, spouting, and water-butt, which will remain green as they are.

About this time we acquired the second dog kennel. We had

brought the terrier's kennel with us, but the spaniel had still no place of his own until Loamy remembered an old kennel which he had used as a chicken coop on his allotment. With the help of a small boy he transported it on a wheelbarrow, doctored it up, and made it waterproof. There are very few wooden kennels in the dale; the cur dogs generally sleep in the barns or small buildings called dog holes attached to them. When it was finished and painted green Geordie came to inspect it. 'Aye, it's a tidy lile dog 'ole,' he said.

Now there only remained the house to set in order. Mrs. Sharples helped us, as she is helping us now with the routine work. We cannot really imagine life in the cottage without her. She comes calmly in, sets things right, and goes again. An author and an artist are strange living-companions; both expect consideration and tolerance when they are busy, and there is no one to give it them but the other harassed partner. Mrs. Sharples, creating a quiet, comfortable atmosphere in the house, smooths away irritation.

Hardy and Chris

THE GATHERING TOGETHER of furniture should be a gradual proceeding, with leisure to consider each piece in relation to the position which it is to occupy, and ample time to wait until the perfect material for curtains or chair coverings appears. But that method could not be indulged in at the beginning of what threatened to be a long war. It was a foregone conclusion that prices would rise and articles become difficult to obtain; and, a cottage without furniture being useless, we were compelled to a speedy buying of necessities. This was a new setting up of a home with few household goods to fall back on, and without the comfortable padding of wedding presents with which married people in similar circumstances would be provided. A typewriter and artist's easels and paraphernalia are poor alternatives to tables, chairs, and crockery.

Having settled such requirements as blankets, sheets, and pans, we bought cream Bolton sheeting for the curtains with the intention of printing it ourselves; but as yet it remains plain. The study, which asked for something more elaborate, has glazed chintz curtains with pale green predominating in the pattern.

For the studio floor we chose natural rush matting, which is attractive to look at, and yet preserves the atmosphere of a working room. We made a plain red rug for this floor, and one in two shades of green for the small bedroom. The rug for the large bedroom then in process of being made is now finished, its pattern influenced by old Norwegian designs.

The rug-making was only possible because of the long evenings at home as a result of the war, and it proved useful to occupy the tedious hours waiting for the All Clear. We bought the wool on one of our hurried shopping expeditions. After choosing it, the rest of the party went to another shop whilst I waited for it to be wrapped. The springy bundles refused to be pressed into shape, and the best that could be made of them were two large ungainly parcels. A boy carried these downstairs, and left them just outside the door, where I waited with them for what cannot have been longer than ten minutes, but seemed double that time. Every second the parcels appeared to grow in size; and I fancied that the hurrying crowds were turning my way and saying: 'Hoarder! Hoarder!' I longed to shout back at them: 'It's

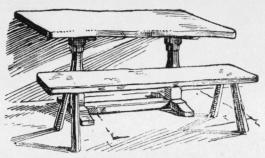

Dining-table and Bench

only wool for rugs. How would you like to have a cottage just ready for furnishing as a war starts?'

We next journeyed to the village of Kilburn in north-east Yorkshire, where Mr. Thompson and the village joiners he has trained make furniture after the tradition of the old craftsmen. If there are many men working in this way in the country we have not heard of them. Our age has produced several specialist firms, but few village craftsmen. We can imagine collectors of a hundred years hence enthusing over a piece of Thompson's furniture with its trade mark of a mouse carved somewhere on it.

We bought two plain single beds with the mouse running along the tops of the feet, mantel-shelves with the mouse carved in relief, chests of drawers with panelled sides, an oak form and stool, bread and cheese boards, some chairs, a working table with plank ends for the studio, and for the dining-room a refectory table whose top, all in one piece, follows the shape of the tree.

A friend once remarked of Kilburn furniture: 'If you think of just what you would like most, Mr. Thompson has it.' A special virtue for us is that its light colouring harmonizes perfectly with our beams. It also fits happily into a room with old furniture; indeed, the combination seems to emphasize the individual beauty of each.

When Geordie looked round the dining-room he remarked that we were 'wick wi' mice.' The carvings are a convenient substitute for toys with young visitors, who amuse themselves going over the house counting them.

A certain amount of furniture came our way in timely fashion. Whilst the cottage was being altered I inherited from an aunt a small Sheraton sideboard, some Georgian silver, a half-moon table, and a pair of Chelsea figures. These all belonged to my

great - great - grandfather, Richard Teed of Devon. We are
familiar with the looks of this gentleman because the family
possesses his portrait and that of his wife, he a round-faced, deter-
mined-looking man, and she a dignified lady in a white dress,
who, before her marriage, was always spoken of as 'pretty Sally

Jenkins of Exeter.' There is a tradition
that the portraits were painted by Sir
Joshua Reynolds, who was a friend of
the sitters, but they are not signed.

For a time Richard Teed designed
and made jewelled swords and sheaths
for George III. In London he lived
in Lancaster Court, Strand; and old
letters tell how members of both
Houses of Parliament met for discussion at his house. The legacies of that
long-dead Georgian gentleman have
settled into the cottage as if they were
made for it, and we like to think that
he would be glad to know that his
treasures are valued in the bleaker north.

We have a friend who declares that all her life she has been a
slave to possessions which have tied her to one place, and kept
her from doing things which she would have enjoyed. She would
like to discard them all, and live in a cottage with nothing more
than 'an up and a down,' and be free. A mansion packed with
heirlooms may be an encumbrance in these days, but a few pieces
of family furniture with their personal connection and their
suggestion of continuity are a joy to possess. Furniture passed
down through many generations has by means of countless
polishings achieved a patina, 'skin' the antique dealers call it,
and an added lustre through its always having been desired and
treasured; perhaps we might unite the two under the word
'aura.'

This is one reason why the buying up of furniture in country
places by dealers has been such a disaster. The mass-produced
modern suites which have so often replaced it are poor sub-
stitutes. For over half a century now dealers have systematically
drained the dales, until there are very few houses with traditional
furniture left. Some realization of this is beginning to be felt,

but the wrong cannot be remedied. Prices at sales are high in normal times, and have increased since the war began. 'These are not for the likes of us,' a local girl about to be married remarked at a sale at which she had hoped to buy something for her new home.

It may be a contradiction, but we must confess that we enjoy antique shops. Those massed collections of furniture and ornaments made before any one now living was born, and which will last long after the youngest among us is dead, have an enormous attraction. Exploring them, we learn to talk glibly of tallboys, court cupboards, kists, of Hepplewhite, Chippendale, Queen Anne. There is a piquant pleasure in acquiring a bargain, particularly nowadays when the occurrence is rare. 'I picked this up for so much,' you say to a visitor, and are gratified at the look of envy on his face.

But it takes time to wear away the impersonal feeling of articles thus obtained. In our collecting we have endeavoured to keep largely to objects which have some connection either with ourselves or with the dale. Many of them came through our friend, Mr. Lodge. He had been living in rooms for some time and had most of his furniture stored in the Assembly Rooms, which belong to him. He suggested that we should choose from there anything that would be useful to us, and house it for him. In this way his furniture would be cleaned and looked after while it helped temporarily to fill our empty spaces. We gratefully accepted his offer, and went down with him to sort over the things.

The Assembly Rooms were built by an ancestor of Mr. Lodge's, old Joseph Lodge, he always calls him, near the end of the eighteenth century for the use of the Friendly Society. They then comprised the only hall in the village, and were in demand for local events until the Temperance Hall took their place and importance. Their very name suggests the leisure of their period, although in this rural place a charitable institution and not the gay life of a spa was their origin.

The building, which is on a miniature scale, has an entrance lobby, a main hall with a gallery at one end, and a vestry or retiring room at the other, and several store-rooms; until 1940, when the soldiers pulled it out, a wooden bench ran round the walls of the main hall. We cherish the hope that in the future the rooms will be utilized again for some village purpose.

On our first visit with Mr. Lodge they presented a scene of picturesque confusion. Chairs, wardrobes, grandfather clocks, tables, chests, bundles of books, old photographs, travelling cases, mingled in the disarray. Worms had bored unchecked into the wood, moths into the padding; and the dust of years lay over everything. The ghostlike objects were relics of a family who had been yeomen in the dales for centuries, and still own property here.

From them we chose a small chest, five chairs in a country Hepplewhite style, and a large oak rocking-chair with a high straight back and short rockers, a type which was fairly common in the dale at one time. Mr. Lodge also presented us with a length of the rail of wooden pegs in the lobby of the Assembly Rooms, so that our coats now hang on the pegs which generations of dalespeople used when they went out for business or entertainment.

Manny brought the furniture up to the cottage in his cart. We watched him coming up the hill, slowly, for he is very considerate of his horse, which is thirty years old. The small cart with its load of graceful chairs jutting out from it at all angles might have been one of those apparitions which are seen for a few minutes on country roads and then vanish. But this was no phantom; it advanced up the green, and the chairs were placed on the flags in front of the cottage to be cleaned before they were taken inside.

Just when we had become used to and fond of the furniture came the order for the billeting of soldiers in the village. Every empty house, every hall and schoolroom was taken, and with them the Assembly Rooms. Mr. Lodge decided that he had no alternative but to sell his furniture by auction. He allowed us to buy the five chairs privately, but felt that the rocking-chair must go in as part of the interest of the sale.

We came up for the event, and arrived during the morning to find the chair, 'grandfather' as we called it, still standing by the fireplace as if the talk of its removal were an idle tale. However, in a few minutes a man drove up in a car, said that it had been overlooked, and took it away. The room seemed strangely bare and wanting without its homely presence. We determined to buy 'grandfather' back whatever he cost.

It was a foregone conclusion that the hall would be packed. Sales are entertainments in the country, and are usually crowded with audiences gathered from long distances. Apart from prospective buyers there are a number of regular habituees whom

Manny brought the Furniture up in his Cart

we see at every sale we attend, and know by their look of familiarity and their knowledge of just how to behave that they will be present at the many we miss. What people buy and what they pay for it, whether prices are high or low, are subjects of conversation for days afterwards.

If the weather makes it at all possible, the actual selling at a house sale is done in the garden or in the space in front of the house. Showers are no deterrent to this outside auctioneering. A crowd of people will be transformed suddenly into a tent of umbrellas, which again disappears at a word from the auctioneer: 'Umbrellas down, please. It's fine again, I think.'

Not coming from a house, Mr. Lodge's furniture was auctioned in the Temperance Hall. It was a happy sale. Instead of the shadow of death which so often hangs over such an occasion, here was Mr. Lodge, hale and hearty, if a little worried by all the arrangements, sitting in the front watching the proceedings. We had been down with him in the morning, and seen the collection displayed in an order which had come miraculously out of the confusion in the Assembly Rooms.

The selling started with the books. Here the few treasures were bundled up with old-fashioned theological works in exquisite leather bindings. We had marked eight leather-bound volumes of Fuller's Works, and, as it was impossible to see from a distance which bundle they were in, we were obliged to bid for all those which looked as if they might contain them. As bundle after bundle was passed down to us we stacked them in the aisle, where late-comers used them for seats. Among them we afterwards found a small leather-bound edition of Pope's Homer.

'Grandfather' came up at last. Unfortunately, the dealers fancied him, and between us the bids rose in quick succession, during which at least once we nodded our heads and bid ourselves up, until he was knocked down to us at £3 5s.

A short lull, and then the quilt came up for sale. It took us by surprise, for there were no catalogues, and in our hurried morning view we had not seen it. All we could make out from the distance was that it was a patchwork quilt of a kind we had wanted for years. When it was finally knocked down to us and handed along the aisle to where we were sitting we found that it was made of silk, which is unusual, with a woolly self-patterned lining. The patches, in lavender, green, grey, cerise, and quaint stripes and floral designs, are arranged in squares and diamonds which also make up the box pattern.

We took our purchases back to the cottage, and 'grandfather' settled himself by the fire as if he had never had that adventurous afternoon, and been in danger of being displayed in an antique shop, and perhaps purchased for a strange house in a strange country.

At the end of the sale we bought the middle part of a huge wardrobe that had been made for Mr. Lodge's father from some of the old pews of the church in the market town; and Loamy has since made this into a good-sized wardrobe. Two of the panels have oval brass plates inscribed with the date 1784 and the names Whaley and Harrison, the owners of the pews. The pine trays of the wardrobe were made into bookshelves of varying sizes to fit our books, and to fill the whole of the back of the recess in the study.

Seeing our enthusiasm about the panelling, Loamy found in his workshop some of the old pews from our own church, and used these as doors for a cupboard in the diningroom. Each door has six panels bordered with scratch moulding, and the top and smallest of these are carved with the date 1676 and the initials of the owners, both churchwardens according to the parish registers, and their wives.

None of these things came easily as new articles would have

Toaster

done. The wardrobe was brought in pieces one chilly day, and left out on the cobbles to be washed. The shelves needed several scrubbings before they were clean enough to be polished with beeswax and turpentine to a velvety smoothness. But the joy of arranging our books on the shelves and setting the wardrobe in place was worth the trouble.

And there were the smaller thrills. So many of these were gifts of Mr. Lodge that his name figures largely in this chapter. He presented us first of all with a pair of bellows on the front of which he had inscribed in brass-headed nails our initials, the name Coleshouse, and the year 1939. Next came a toaster, a steel contraption standing on three legs with five two-pronged toasting forks and a steel ring which swivels round to hold the

D

plate—a museum piece, this.   An oak spoon-box and rack was really an exchange for a portrait which the artist drew of him. Later we received the fire-irons for the study, and a 'wag bi t' wall' clock, which is after the style of a Dutch wall clock, with a face arched at the top and decorated with brilliantly painted roses and the weights for winding hanging down the wall below it.   They will be for all our lives reminders of his interest and friendship.

Those were exciting moments when Mr. Lodge opened his queer-shaped parcels; but all his visits have had some interest. Sometimes he brought an old book of poems to show us, a rush-light holder or a candle snuffer found amongst his treasures; sometimes he told of an interesting entry which he had discovered in the parish registers, or informed us of a recent village wedding or birth.

We have mentioned the treasures which the blacksmith brought to the house.   The eternity knocker, which graces our yard door and at which we gaze when we have our meals outside, was the gift of Loamy, who dug it up in his garden.   Knitting sheaths made additions to our collection; and the gifts from our home people and many others we cherish both for themselves and the thought behind them.

All of them help to make the house into a home.   They blend with each other and with the furniture, as comfort and style blend in an old cottage made livable for to-day.

WHEN, having taken our place in the line of owners and tenants of the cottage, we wished to learn all we could of our predecessors, the old deeds provided a basis for our search.

Names on old deeds are like those on old tombs. We know that they belonged to real people wanting happiness and the experiences of life, but they are dim to us because we can only surmise the details of their days, their personal standards and aspirations. They present for the most part ordinary unrecorded people, too far from our own time for their reputations to have survived. We do not know whether they were generous or mean, lively or sedate, brave or cowardly; they are reduced to mere names.

The yellow parchments, with their elaborate writing and seals and marks for signatures, showed us names which are still common in the dale. By delving in the parish registers we brought more life into the dead letters, and realized as actual people those who in varying degrees have left their stamp on the building and its history. As we came nearer the present time it was easier to learn more, for, like most houses in the dales, the cottage is identified with its past tenants in the minds of the villagers.

We have no record of when Coleshouse was built, so that the men who laid the first stones are almost as vague and obscure as those who constructed the Iron Age dwellings on the southern slopes of the hill which we face. The names Kirk Close for a field at this end of the village, and Cross Well for a spring in it, seem to indicate an early church; we like to imagine people going from our corner round the green to services in a simple building by the beck, and that this happened through the centuries until the later church was built on a site at the west end. This implies the existence of wattle and daub or turf huts before the present buildings, an implication justified by the presence of what look like ancient foundations in the fields, an indefinable sensation of long settlement, and the name Abbey Garth, which suggests that the pasture behind the cottage was the property of one of the Yorkshire monasteries, probably Jervaulx. Perhaps Coleshouse was once a herdsman's hut.

These are, however, pleasant if not impossible fancies. The

name of the cottage brings us a little nearer reality; if it came from that George Cole who held property in the district it would be built in the early years of the seventeenth century. But the first recorded information we have is the mention in a deed of 1741 of an earlier indenture, when Jane Lambert of Marsett sold the property to Robert Morton, of Linend in Kildwick parish, in 1699.

Marsett, a remote hamlet at the head of the Raydale valley, rests under the fells which mark our horizon from the cottage windows. It is scattered along one end of a stretch of common land on which at a single time cows, horses, sheep, geese, ducks, and hens may be seen grazing. A beck bounding it on the north side is crossed by a bridge which makes a definite entrance to a place that has still the semblance of a medieval village.

If we think of most of the present houses and barns as lower buildings thatched with ling, we form a picture not unlike what the Marsett of 1699 must have been when the widow, Jane Lambert, who lived there, sold this property at Town Head. We imagine her coming down to our village, which was then the most important place in the upper dale, to arrange for the sale, with the flowing skirts of her kirtle thickly gathered at the waist, and a hood with a cape attached drawn round her head and shoulders. On her way she would pass two or three recently built houses with stone-slated roofs, conspicuous in their newness among the darker buildings. Perhaps she trudged through snow, for it was December. Lambert was then a common name in Raydale. Some branches of the family were of the educated yeoman class; we hear of a John Lambert of Marsett journeying to London at the beginning of the century.

Robert Morton occupied the house himself after he bought it, for the parish registers record his death in Askrigg in 1716. His son, George Morton, who sold it again in 1741 for £7 5s., was a shoe-maker. Poverty may have obliged him to part with the property, for his son died in the poorhouse soon after the death of the father.

The new owner was a Christopher Caygill, whose family retained it for ninety-nine years. The name Caygill is a magic one here, for it revives the long story of the clockmaking industry, which began at the end of the seventeenth century and ended within living memory. It was a flourishing craft in the days of large families, when a grandfather's clock was considered one of the few necessary pieces of furniture for every bride.

All through the clockmaking history one name stands out above the rest for a generation or two, and its successor usually has a link with the earlier one, for apprentices were apt to fall in love with their masters' daughters. The development of brass and painted faces can be traced, and relics of both kinds ornament many cottage and farm-house kitchens. As I write I can hear, through the open door of the neighbouring cottage, a thin piercing note as a clock made by John Pratt strikes the hour.

A Caygill Clock-face

By rights this should be a Caygill clock, for the mistress of the cottage was descended from the clockmaker of that name. There are probably a number of his clocks in the dale still, but the only one we have seen is in a house about a mile away. The artist has drawn the brass face engraved with a swan and the maker's name.

Christopher Caygill, who died in 1803 and was followed by his son, was an early and an outstanding maker. We should like to think that the clockmaker owned our cottage, and lived here and worked under the window in the little room which is now our hall, but throughout the eighteenth century there were at least two distinct branches of Caygills with a Christopher at the head, and each of these with sons and grandsons called Christopher. Their propensity for this name 'has smothered them in confusion. Christenings, marriages, and deaths of members of their families are on every page of the parish registers. Our searches in these, and in the will which John Caygill, a farmer, made in 1803, compel us to admit the likelihood of our predecessors having been farmers; but even if the sound of the clockmaker's tools did not echo within these walls, we can safely assume that he at least entered them at times to visit relatives.

It was during the Caygills' century of ownership that the name of the cottage was altered from Coleshouse to Crabtree. If a crab-apple tree influenced them in making the change that has long since disappeared. The Adam style of the bedroom fireplace also suggests that they raised the building, and replaced the thatched roof with stone slates and the small mullioned windows with larger frame ones.

It was again a Christopher Caygill who sold Coleshouse in 1840. He was then living lower down the dale; Betty Terry, who bought it, did not live in it herself; and from then until our time its occupants were tenants. Betty Terry died in 1885; and her property was scattered amongst many people. This cottage came to her second cousin, who was then a child, and who sold it to us in 1938.

When Miss Betty Terry made her will in 1880 the tenant was a Mr. Jimmy Trotter, a farmer and bacon curer. The lean-to was built for him, and he used it chiefly for salting bacon and hams. Old people, recollecting visits to him and his wife, tell of seeing these hanging to dry on hooks on the kitchen ceiling. These hooks had vanished when we came, but they account for the numerous large holes which we found in the beams.

Jimmy's wife, Mary Ann, was famous through the dale for her Wensleydale cheese. We picture her moving down the dairy every morning to turn the cheeses which she had placed to dry on the narrow shelves. Jimmy Trotter was her second husband. Her first had been a Walker; her maiden name was Sunter, which could easily be made to sound like 'saunter,' and she used to say: 'When I wed again I'll get a galloper.' The drawing on page 12, taken from an old photograph, shows her a typical dales-woman, with a milk can on one arm, a basket of butter or cheese on the other, and a back-can strapped over her shoulders, ready to start out to milk her cows in the pastures at the lower end of the village. Later she moved with Jimmy to a larger farm, and after he died she lived in a cottage by the school. Her strong individual character has caused her to be remembered vividly by all kinds of people.

The same might be said of Jimmy. He was very jealous of his farm land; if he saw a dog cross his pasture he would complain to the owner. He disliked trespassing boys even more than dogs. Every now and again he would walk into the day school, and ask if he might say something. He was a tall man, with blue eyes, and he spoke with a lisp.

'Now, Mr. Watson,' he would begin, 'some o' your boys 'a' been gittin' ower intiv my pastur, an' Ah 've cu' to tell 'em that Ah weea't hev it. If Ah finnd 'em at it ageean Ah sall tak' t' case to Leyburn.'

He put a wooden gate, painted green, between the stable and the old buildings to keep his calves and pigs from straying, and he printed on this 'Sneck gate' as a terse reminder to the neighbours who fetched water from his well. He had as great a pride in the garden as in the farm, and his tenancy marked one of its periods of prosperity. He pruned and tended the two plum-trees which grew on the house walls, and were then in their prime.

Some tenants had anxious times when the plums were ripening. An old dalesman tells how as a boy he once helped to steal some of them.

'Ah minnd when Ah war a lad tweea folk lived i' t' cottage, an' when t' plums war ripe yan on 'em allus stayed i' t' hoose for fear o' t' lads gitten 'em. But yar neet beeath war oot togither, an' Ah an' anither lad, Pete Metcalfe, t' blacksmith's son, ga'ed for t' plums. He war taller nor me, so Ah stood on t' grund, an' 'e climmed on to ma shoulders, an' we filled wer pockets wi' plums till they were nigh burstin'. Fun on it was that as we went up t' lane we met 'em cu'in' doon, an' they knew naught, nor nivver did know who 'd takken 'em. Ah doubt we sud n'a' done it,' he finishes, 'but they were ower anxious—near folk. They nivver gi'ed owt away i' thar lives.'

A postman and his wife were later tenants. 'Aye, 'twas a funny old cottage,' his wife told us, 'but I liked living there. Many an hour I 've sat on yond wall, and watched t' carts starting up t' hill with oil and produce for Gunnerside i' Swaledale.'

The couple now live less than two miles away across the valley; but when the postman passed by this spring it was the first time he had come this way for many years. He stood back and looked at the house, and delivered an oration to the green, which was deserted.

'Eh, look at t' owd 'ouse! What a change! And t' outbuilding—three winders in it. And t' kitchen—three winders too. An' t' owd stable an' all. Well, I never! What an improvement! Who would 'a' thought it possible?' And, still marvelling, his voice dwindled away out of hearing.

Unlike the house, our road retains many names in constant use. Among others it is in parts Moor Road, Stony Bank Foot, Muker Road, and Faith Hill. Faith was the name of an old lady who lived in the last farm-house, and who was so outstanding in her generation that the road was called after her, and will probably continue to be called Faith Hill long after the reason for its name is forgotten. Faith, Mary Ann, Jimmy, three characters living within speaking distance of each other; and now it would be hard to find many more than that number in the whole village.

Life is to some extent duller and more stereotyped without these village characters. Hearing of them we could wish that it were possible to sit round the fire and listen to their opinions on matters of to-day and their apt retorts. But in regretting them we are inclined to forget that not all were kind and humorous or even decent according to present-day standards. Grappling with nature in its wildest and grimmest aspects did not make for gentleness. A man could be ruthless in his animosity to another.

If we are softer and less individual in these days we have not lost that 'neighbourly obligation' which is so often lacking in the towns. There is still kindness to people in trouble, and still overflowing hospitality. Sociability compensates for lack of entertainments, and we have much visiting amongst each other, especially on Sundays, which are considered dull days if no one calls. It is seldom that a person going on an errand to a dales house is not invited inside.

A lady speaking about the cottage said: 'Somehow it 's been a house that 's always had a lot of visitors.'

Coleshouse under our rule has kept up that tradition. Visitors have come to call, or for the day, or for longer stays. Sometimes they have followed each other so closely as almost to form a procession. All of them have echoed in their various ways that first opinion of our neighbour's: 'It 's nice living.'

PART TWO

A YEAR IN THE COTTAGE

We cut our own peats, . . . without distant trafficking
—W. G. COLLINGWOOD

IN THE FIRST THREE MONTHS of 1941 our visits to the cottage were so frequent that we seemed to be already here. We were occupied with preparations; but our chief impression of that time is of the valley locked in winter.

In the intense cold which held the land in its grip human beings and their domestic animals seemed the only living things. Of the wild creatures which had not hibernated for the winter many had died. The vegetable life was stiff and brittle, as if it would break when touched. The hill masses, having lost the heat conserved during the summer, now seemed to reflect and intensify the penetrating cold.

We thought of other Januaries in the dales. One in Bishopdale when the hills were sprinkled with frozen snow which became tinted to a delicate pink in the pale sunset. It was exhilarating to walk on the hard, dry roads between the glittering hills. Then one morning the sky grew heavy and more snow was predicted; but instead, we wakened to a green valley and mud in the place of frozen ground. Flocks of fieldfares arrived to feed in the meadows. Farmers took advantage of the mild weather to spread the heaps of 'muck.'

The abrupt weakening of the strength of winter, as if a clenched hand had suddenly tired and let go, brings a sense of liberation. It does not always happen in the night; we saw and felt it one January day in Swaledale. As we crossed the bridge over the river the waterfalls were arrested cascades of ice, and long icicles made crystal decorations in the ravine. An hour later the spell broke; icicles dropped with a tinkling sound on to the rocks; water rolled over the solid cascades; and a drizzling rain began to fall. Visibly the valley softened and relaxed.

We have been snowed up in Wharfedale in January in a storm which raged unceasingly for two days until roads were impassable, telegraph poles fell, and all communication with the outer world was lost. But on that occasion as soon as the storm abated the snow began to thaw, and water and slush ran down the slopes as if unseen hands were sweeping it from the fells into the river.

On all these other Januaries the wintriness had come and gone, but this year it stayed. It was not quite so intense perhaps as it had been the previous January, but there was more snow. Each day a fresh fall spread a new layer which the frost hardened on to the rest. The cold, creeping down like a living creature, numbed hands and feet, froze the becks, gripped the land.

The mason went from house to house helping to thaw pipes which froze again immediately the heat was withdrawn.

'Are ta frozzen?' 'How's t' watter?' ''Es ta anny bursts?' were once more the regular questions.

As fast as the paths were swept they were covered again. We trudged through thick snow to the village, where the trodden roads and pavements were coated with hard, thick ice. Mrs. Chapman, carrying a pail from her doorway, found herself on her back with the pail over her head, and was lucky to escape with a shaking. After slipping and falling as he went down the street, Mr. Lodge kept indoors for weeks because of the state of the roads. Slight thaws flooding the surface with water which quickly froze again made matters worse.

We thought of the dalesman's inevitable remark to visitors who praise his country: 'Aye, it's all right i' summer, but you want to be here i' winter.'

We were enclosed in the fastness of the valley, divided from Swaledale by barriers of snowdrifts, for in these days the moor road is not cut through like the more important Buttertubs Pass.

Bad roads and dark nights prevented journeys up and down the dale. To the countryman winter presents a far bigger contrast to the summer than it does to the townsman. Nature, not gangs of workmen, must disperse most of the snow here.

It was exhilarating to experience winter thus in this northern climate, to brace ourselves against it and breathe the clean, cutting air, to battle with swirling blizzards, to struggle up the moor road by planting our feet in the deep footprints made by the farmers as they went up to fodder their sheep, until an enormous white cliff towered up to bar the way. Often the deep snow was so hard that we walked on the surface without sinking.

There were dull days, but there were also days of surpassing beauty when snow and sun combined to make a scene of magic. On a few rare occasions a delicate glassy coating appeared on the snow as if a thick crystal growth had sprouted from the solid white mass. Bunches of bents and rushes standing above the rest were transformed into tall glass plants hung with crystal fringes. On those days the sun shone with intense brilliance from a blue sky, and the whole landscape glittered in it. Shades on the pure white changed from greyish blues to pale greens and purples, until, as afternoon wore on, the ethereal tones were lost in the warmth of an alpine glow. It was an experience to be grasped and held, for it was so fleeting; with the slightest rise in a still freezing temperature the brittle crystals fell back on to the snow.

The artist caught some of these pictures in drawings of crayon, a medium which expressed the delicacy of the subject. The colours came with the sun. On dull days under a grey sky the white world was only relieved by the brown house walls and the bare tree branches. There was no green.

Three geese in a pasture up the moor road looked down at the frozen water of the beck in which they were used to drink, and then stood motionless as if they too were frozen to the ground; and only the yellow tinge of their plumage and the orange dabs of beaks and feet marked them out from their cold white background.

It was good on those days to turn into the cottage and be met by the warmth from the radiator pipes. The building stood the winter well. No damp blemish marked the plaster in the upper rooms. This was more of a cause for satisfaction than may be at first obvious. Thickly falling snow, like heavy rain, does not

There were Days of Surpassing Beauty

penetrate the stone roofs, but light dry snow, coming in a blizzard, is driven between the slates. This settles in the underdrawing, and if left soaks through the ceiling as it melts. In one of the winter's blizzards there was scarcely a house in which snow did not accumulate in this manner. It was carried away in pailfuls; the record for one house as far as we heard was forty pails.

The storms, giving ample warning of their coming, did not occasion so many overblown sheep as in some less severe seasons. It allowed time to bring the flocks down to the lower pastures. A horse which was wintering on the moor was lost for several days. After the first heavy fall of snow the owner 'went up to lait it, and couldn't finnd it.' He spent some hours searching for it, prodding under the walls as they do for sheep, and then had to leave it. It was found a few days later by a man who noticed its ears sticking up out of a shake hole, and, except for being slightly weak on its legs for a few hours, it suffered no harm.

Roads and hilly fields were turned into toboggan runs. We could see several from the cottage door. Dark forms waiting or climbing up the slope stood out in the snow like figures in a Breughel scene. The moor road made a magnificent run. The children dragged their sledges a mile up it; the tracks they made were visible for as far as we were able to walk. Riding down they reached a tremendous pace which was accelerated by the final steep bend just above the cottage. Cuthbert knocked at the door and asked if we had any nails to mend his sledge. We found him a few and some pieces of wood, and helped him to repair the sledge, and a quarter of an hour later he raced past the green on it.

The long frost brought to the old people memories of similar winters when they were young.

'Manny a time Ah 've seen t' moor road when we walked on t' wall tops for weeks,' Geordie said.

But more than heavy snowstorms, which, after all, are not unusual, the old people remember when they used the frozen river as a roadway. Geordie skated down it many times. An old lady tells of skating the six miles to the market town for six consecutive weeks.

There were skating parties on Semerwater with bonfires burning on the shores. We have so far missed an experience in life in not having seen a bonfire burning by a frozen lake. The combination of ice and fire offers to be melodramatic. There were nights and days this winter when it would have been pleasant to linger by a glowing fire, when hoar frost settled on landscape and people alike, whitening clothes and hair so that we seemed to have gone back to the fashion of powdered locks. We have not yet even skated on Semerwater. The moorland beauty drew us too long in the limited time left from other duties, and when we finally arranged to go thaw intervened.

The last snowstorm was the heaviest when winter showed that it still had power. The large woolly flakes fell silently until windows were covered and the yard was a high solid block which had to be cut through to make a way from the back door. It was days before the road on our side of the valley was cleared for traffic, and several more before a car could get up the moor road as far as the green. The people who have their coal delivered by the Durham lorry had to do without for three weeks.

The mud that followed the snow decided us to buy clogs for work in the garden. We were measured for them in the shop in the market town, and the cobbler delivered them when he came on his rounds. The artist wears hers gaily, but I have not yet been able to prevent mine from rubbing my ankles raw. Clogs have one disadvantage for gardening in that they are inclined to fill up with soil, but nothing else keeps the feet so warm and dry. The farmer on the hill behind us wears them for working, and sometimes refuses to take them off when he comes down to the village, a habit that is a great trouble to his wife. 'Thoo'll be clatterin' doon t' street i' thy clogs,' she says.

Whilst we were in the shop several soldiers came in for tiny children's clogs in red or blue leather. Most of them were sending the coloured shoes as presents to their children in Scotland. We were immediately reminded of Chintah, and ordered a blue pair for her.

Chintah was our first experience of a refugee. Her coming brought to mind that Saturday, the day before war was declared, when we drove car loads of bewildered evacuees, expectant mothers, and mothers with children smeared with the chocolate with which they had been presented, to householders equally perplexed about receiving them. They were many of them so transitory as to be impersonal; indeed, our last work was to drive several families back home the same night.

But Chintah was permanent. From the agonies of a flight from Belgium and nights spent in shelters in London this three-year-old child was to be received at a village four miles from the cottage. For a few days at a stage in her journey she was our special charge. Whilst we were still at home with our families we received an urgent message from Miss Dyke, the lady who had promised to take her, asking us if we would meet a child in Barnsley and keep her until we were coming up the dale again. She was travelling with two elderly people to whom a Quaker lady had offered a home.

We drove to the station at which the refugees were to arrive, picked out the lady on the platform, and with her watched the train come in. No elderly people or small child alighted. We met other trains; we stood in offices while the railway authorities telephoned here and there; but there was no news of them. The Quaker lady took us home to have some tea and discuss what we should do, and she left us there in case they arrived unexpectedly while she went down to meet the last possible train that night. She displayed no alarm, no irritation, no worry. And she found them on that last train, as somehow we felt she would. Owing to the bombing, they had arrived at the wrong station in London and had come by another route.

Chintah sat, a forlorn little figure clutching a doll, in a corner of the back seat while every one helped the elderly couple and collected parcels and cases. We took her to our car and started the slow journey back in the dusk. We were pleased that the child sat contentedly nursing her doll, which she called Sossie, for we had hurriedly read a letter from the society in whose care she had spent the previous night and which said that she was quite good during the day but cried persistently for her mother at bedtime.

We managed to overcome that difficulty, and Chintah, finding our home a haven after storms, became attached to us. She would go anywhere with us, but always at the gate of a fresh house she planted her feet firmly on the ground, and looking up at us said: 'We're not going to live here.' She was a fascinating and unusual child, partly through a mixture in her of many races, a complication which barred her from benefiting from the Government evacuation schemes. She was one of many who must thank the Society of Friends for its broad-mindedness in such cases. Her father is interned in France. The mother managed to escape from Belgium to England with her two children, the younger of whom, a baby boy, is now in a nursery school.

About a week later we brought Chintah up to her new home. This time our paraphernalia included a bundle of fruit-trees packed in a borrowed trailer. The child, sensing another strange house, was very quiet on her journey, and wept bitterly when we parted from her. But she soon settled down in her new home, and in those early months of 1941 she came often with Miss Dyke to have tea with us at the cottage.

Perhaps the happiest visit was during the first week in January when there was still some festive feeling. We could not buy a real Christmas tree, but we found in Miss Banks's shop a little arti-ficial one in a red pot, and we hung this with coloured lights to form a gay decoration on the table. Miss Banks's shop is of the type which sells everything, and it also provided us with a large frosted bell with the inscription 'A Happy Xmas.' This was sold to us in December on condition that we did not take it until after Christmas when its use as a shop decoration would be over, an arrangement which suited both sides that season. We all drew presents from a cotton-wool house, and played Ring o' Roses till the room whirled round us.

The soldiers brought unusual life and movement to the village in those worst winter months. Their lusty voices, singing or talking, came from the billets; small groups of them drilled in the road above the church; scattered units in brilliant-coloured shorts and shirts sped past the cottage windows at the start or the end of running exercises; and always one or two fully armed men stood beating their hands to keep out the piercing cold while they guarded the lorries in the market-place or the small space at the bottom of the moor road. Their presence gave a sense of security during those dark months.

The men of a Scottish regiment settled in first, and captivated the village by their charm and lively spirits. They were followed by another regiment, and that again by another. If by the end of the winter the village as a whole was less welcoming to the soldiers, it was only because they wearied of the continual getting to know the men and then losing them. All through those months dances and whist drives were weekly occurrences. Soldiers and evacuees doubled the village population, and the electric company had to install another engine.

A picture of that time stands out in our minds of a convoy ranged up one side of the village street in preparation for starting out on a day's manœuvres. The long line of drably coloured vehicles with sinister-looking guns jutting from them, standing on the white frozen road with the snow-covered fells as a background, had a strange un-English aspect. Enclosed in the street, they seemed like visitants from another world, and were a stirring if a sobering sight.

In those months the most frequent knockers at the door were the Kirkbride children. 'Do you want any kindling?' they would ask, and pile the chips on the step.

The thaw coming gradually revealed the green valley again; but, as if to remind us of the long winter, masses of snowdrops sprang up under the trees by the river.

The Tarn

THERE WAS LITTLE but the longer days to distinguish spring this year from a mild winter. Sharp east winds cut our faces, and seemed to penetrate into every fibre of our being. A warmer day bringing hope of others was followed by cold which seemed keener in comparison. The trees remained bare. The weather was a chilly background to our final arrival with the ill-fated trailer, and our unremitting painting activities.

'Is 't as caud as this whar you cu' fra?' Geordie asked.

'No, not quite,' we said.

'Whya,' he replied, 'Ah think ye 've changed your fiddle for a gewgah.'

We asked him what a gewgaw was, and he imitated playing a Jew's harp.

The cold brought one advantage in that we were able to ignore the garden completely, for it would have been useless to sow seeds in the starved earth. We reminded ourselves that in this high northern climate we must add on a month to gardening dates, most of which are designed for southern counties. The long light days seemed to be wasting themselves away.

Rain, giving a preparatory soaking to the gardens and a start to the grass, would have been some consolation, but no rain came. The moisture drained off the steep pastures, and dry winds turned the peaty soil to powder. Growth was suspended. Only the rhubarb plants poked pink and yellow shoots through the ground; we covered ours with any old buckets we could find to force them. And under the hoary thorn hedge a single primrose plant bloomed so richly that it looked as though a massed bunch of those flowers had been placed there.

But even while we shivered there were signs of spring. A curlew calling across the pastures and black-headed gulls flying over the cottage on their way from the river announced the return of the moor birds. Day after day we saw them until we could no longer resist the call of the fells and the tarn, whose cold grey water through all the year is a magnet drawing us to it. It was good now to stride out in the brisk air and gain new strength and vigour.

As we walked over the heather and peat hags, grouse, having clung to their nests as long as they dared, rose uttering their hoarse rattling cry. We found a golden plover's nest neatly filled with its four mottled eggs. Golden plovers, being shy birds, are not so often seen as their cousins the green plovers, but they haunt particular stretches of the moor, where they will stand motionless on rocks or tufts of heather for long periods. Aloof and handsome in their golden plumage, they might be called the aristocrats of the moor. Just as their plumage loses itself in the heather and bents, so their melancholy whistling note might be the wind in the crags. A few weeks later in the year the spaniel scented a baby plover in the wiry grass, and stood patiently waiting to show us his find. For a moment we held in our hands the downy creature, which at this age is, more than most moor birds, a miniature of its parents.

Curlews and plovers are seldom startled on the nest. Long before an alien creature has approached they swoop above and endeavour by their angry cry to entice the intruder in another direction. It is the heavier birds which are more easily taken unawares. We almost stepped on a teal's nest before the drake rose and darted swiftly away from us and out of sight; its brilliant blue-green plumage shimmered as it was caught in a gleam of sun. The nine eggs lay in a basket-like nest of grass and rushes at our feet.

The black-headed gulls flying over it marked the site of the tarn from a distance, and their excited cries increased as we approached. The majority of nests were in the reeds which run in a long strip parallel with the shore, but there were a few, mere

hollows in tufts of long grass or rushes, on the boggy edges. This
being the beginning of the nesting season there was not more
than a single egg in each.

The gulls started to nest at the tarn some years ago, and their
number is increasing. But gulls are capricious in their choice
of haunts, and each spring we wonder whether they will return.
There is no fish in the water to add to their insect diet; but the
birds frequent the becks and continually through the day make
journeys to the rivers in the valleys on either side. This year
they took full advantage of the newly ploughed fields which the
exigencies of war have caused.

The smaller birds pursued their quiet way, undisturbed by
the noise and bustle of the self-important gulls. Two sandpipers
ran busily to and fro on a rocky promontory, while a dunlin
perched at the end of it and gazed fixedly at the water. When
we had sat quite still on the heather for a time the noise of the
gulls lessened as a few settled on their nests.

There is a sense of mystery about any mountain tarn. A
lake nestles under the hills which supply its water, but a tarn
stretched on the summit is filled from unseen sources. Its
surface mirrors the blue summer heavens, but the more general
grey skies or the flying clouds of storms best reflect its spirit.
It symbolizes tracts remote from man and claimed by wild
creatures as their own. For them there is infinite variety in the
miniature creeks where the young ones can swim, in the islands
which form hunting-places, and in the mud or pebbles of the
beaches, whether the water laps gently on the shores or rolls in
waves across the whole stretch. Man is an alien here, and there
is no real peace whilst he remains. Yet the tarn owes its present
size to the work of man, for it was enlarged to serve as a dam for
the lead mines lower down the next valley.

However much the warmth delayed, it was pleasant because it
was spring, and in the dales we welcome spring not only for itself
but for what it promises. When Mr. Bell called this year to
collect for the Red Cross sale he sat down by the fire and talked
in his own particular way, which is slowly and with many pauses,
as if he turned each sentence over in his mind before he uttered it,
a habit which gives a certain weight to his remarks. We talked
about Snaizeholme, a remote valley higher up the dale where
numbers of little becks run down the hill-sides to join the larger

one in the valley, and old tracks lead to the few farms scattered in the basin. Mr. Bell went to one of these when he was a young man, and lived alone in his house until he married a girl from one of the other farms.

'It must have been splendid living there,' we said.

Mr. Bell considered for a moment, and then he agreed: 'Aye, it's very nice wi' all them little becks i' t' spring o' t' year.'

There was a Chaucerian flavour about that remark, an echo of life lived close to the land. We repeat it often to ourselves for joy in the words. 'Aye, it's very nice wi' all them little becks i' t' spring o' t' year.' Perhaps that valley brings out the latent poetry in a man. The name itself is poetry—Snaizeholme, the holm among the twigs.

On 25th April, the spring term, new tenants came to a farm in the hamlet, a move which involved the interchanging of many families. The smaller farms, which are the most numerous and which vary in size and quality, are continually changing tenants. A young man often starts on a remote farm as Mr. Bell did. If things go well the stages in his life will be a high farm, a lower better one, sometimes a third and still better one, and finally retirement to a house in the village or hamlet. The sheep are heughed to the farm where they know the moor and will not stray, and are valued at each change of tenancy.

Standing for long hours painting the windows we noted the number of farmers who go up and down the moor road. Some of these live in ordinary houses in the village, for, though there are what we call the settled farms with barns and buildings round the homestead, it is possible to run a successful farm completely detached from the house, provided there is the proper balance between meadow and pasture and sheep gaits on the moor.

The smallest of these are often made up of odd pieces of land, a pasture here, two meadows there. Of the pastures which line the green tracks one is rented by one man, the next by another, and so on right along the way.

There is a story of a farming village in northern Norway whose coasts were suddenly visited by herring shoals in the season. One of the inhabitants persuaded the people to sell their land to build houses and factories, and so share in the prosperity which the herring fishing would bring. When all the land was built on except that of one farmer, who would have nothing to do with the scheme, the herring shoals failed to come that way, and the people, faced with ruin and famine, looked with despair at the useless buildings occupying their precious ground. The food which one farm could produce was not enough for all. There is sufficient resemblance between that country and this for the same lesson to apply. The land as land is vital to the community.

The many barns, each one serving two or three fields, make this system of farming possible. Housing cattle on the ground floor and storing hay above, they form with their groups of fields self-contained units. The stone buildings, which look to have grown from the earth, give an air of permanency to the landscape as if they had always been there and always would be. They reflect the changes in the weather as the hills do. As I write a streak of sunlight has caught one on Croft Hill so that it and the leafless sycamore beside it stand out clearly against the filmy sky. The gleam does not reach the second barn, which seems to be fading into the grey clouds. Nor would the moor road be the same without the two barns which stand with their sheltering trees on either side of it where the road forks. The barns, lathes as we call them, proclaim the story of the valley as much as does the ruined castle down the dale.

Strangers remark on their numbers. When Chintah's mother and aunt came to see her this summer it was their first visit to the north; and, though they were working as land girls in Sussex, they had never before come across anything like our barns. As on their journey they saw them dotting the hill-sides they could not imagine what they were for, and finally decided that they were houses.

'Yes,' said one, 'but if they are houses where are the windows?'

'Perhaps they are at the other side out of the way of the weather,' suggested the other.

Then they passed barns of which they could see both sides, and, coming to the conclusion that the narrow air slits must be the only means of light, they felt that they had really arrived at the dour stark north.

The lambs which now began to dot the fields with white came into a cold world. The swallows trustingly arrived, and built under the eaves of an old barn across the road. The North Riding tractor came to break up the land allotted for ploughing; it was sad to see the grass go before it in this essentially grazing country. The farmers, benefiting by the experience of the 1914-

1918 war, when the corn never ripened in this high region, were
to plant chiefly kale and mixed crops for silage.

One evening we took a friend up Raydale and to the shores of
Semerwater, and, sitting on the rocks with the water soughing
at our feet, let the peace and isolation lay their benison on our
souls. A moorhen sped across the surface as if it had suddenly
realized the lateness of the hour. The soft cooing voices of the
birds suggested that as night came on they accepted us as friends.
Darkness creeping slowly down folded to itself the ruins of the
church above the lake, a crude but characterful little church
which the inhabitants built at their own cost and by their own
labour. In its shadow the dalespeople come still to their final rest.

About this time the dogs developed the habit of waiting for
Geordie when he came out on his way to feed the hens. They
lie on the green, and as the old man emerges with his pail hung on
his arm and his hand grasping the lapel of his coat they rise
expectantly. He speaks to them in the low voice which deaf
people so often use: 'Hardy, lile dog,' 'Well, Chris,' and then
he digs his trowel into the mash and brings out a small lump of
it for each dog. He bends down to give it to them, very slowly,
for long hours shepherding on the fells in wet and stormy weather
have stiffened his joints.

Geordie's pail is as much a part of him as the old thick coat he
wears for the journey. When the artist sketched him he looked
for a long time at the finished picture.

'It's good, isn't it?' said a friend who happened to be there.

'Aye,' said Geordie, 'pail's ta'en weel, but t' other's a funny
awd boy. Neeabody'd ken it, wad they?'

One day the carrier drove his cart on to the green, lifted a
seat off it and placed it on the grass. Then we knew that however spring delayed summer was round the corner. During the
few real summer weeks elderly holiday makers rested on it for a
little while; and one Sunday morning a few men, deserting the
more popular seat at the foot of the moor road, drifted to it
to discuss the affairs of the dale and the world. Conversation
soon turned on the war and what was wrong with the running of it.
We are a democratic community, and it is certain that few of us
would survive many weeks of totalitarian rule.

In the packhorse days a string of jagger ponies used to be
brought down from the high track which was once the main way
up the valley; and their loads of coal were deposited on the green,

where the farmers and village people came with carts to buy it. At a sale a few weeks ago we bought a collar that was worn by a leader of a packhorse train. It is a broad leather band hung with seven good-sized round brass bells engraved with a pattern and the initials WR.

Suddenly the cold passed, and it was spring at its loveliest. The wild daffodils peeped out round the well, shyly in this their first year. Early and late spring flowers blossomed together in riotous confusion. We picnicked with some friends camping in one of the gills. Their clearing in the wood by the beck was a bower of flowers, primroses and forget-me-nots, cowslips and oxlips, bluebells and wood anemones, and in one secluded corner herb paris. The blackthorn trees were great white pompoms, and the bird cherries giant bouquets. We found a willow warbler's nest on a hill-side, and a spotted flycatcher's cupped by a piece of bark in the fork of a tree. A low stone ivy-hung building under a crag whose rock formed its back might in its solitary hidden position have been a hermit's cell.

The warm days brought old Mrs. Kirkbride out to the garden to tend the flower-beds round the edges and in the grass. In the market town the nursery stalls were the most popular feature. Farmers' wives sorted out plants for the borders. We tried to ignore the stalls, for gifts from other gardens had already filled our limited space, but we succumbed to the joy of buying bunches of pansies.

The sycamore buds burst; in the lane by the hamlet sweet cicely filled the air with the strong aroma of aniseed; we heard the cuckoo and saw two small hedge sparrows chase one from the bush where they had built their nest. The cows came out into the pastures. It was really spring.

The Cobbles

WHILST THE COLD SPELL still lasted we turned to the garden. Working in it, we discovered that we had not fully appreciated the joy of ownership until we had actually dug, sown, and harvested on our own property, and had overcome the difficulties and made use of the advantages of our soil and site. Having done that, we felt we had become a part of it as it was a part of the countryside.

Our instinct on our few stays the previous year had been to ignore everything else and set to work on uprooting the nettles, an instinct shared by our visitors, who, if there were thick gloves and a fork handy, were often found stabbing viciously at a chosen patch. The nettles grew in deadly clusters under the hedge and the walls, and were the main crop in the end garden. The venomous leaves stung us as we made a way to the old gooseberry bushes or picked the few stray raspberries, and left us with tingling legs and fingers for the rest of the day. Surely no weed gives such joy in its eradication as the nettle. You dig out and destroy not only the visible plant but a gnarled straggling root from which innumerable other malicious shoots would spring. Now that we were here permanently we could tackle the job in earnest.

In places the artist liked the weeds, and insisted on keeping the nettles under the ash saplings, which in local opinion should themselves be removed from a vegetable garden. She also wished to leave the woundwort round the well, and the white dead nettles under the south wall. In full bloom these were so beautiful that we gathered bunches of them for the house; but they could not be allowed to grow unchecked, or why call it a garden?

It is scarcely possible to keep a wild effect in any part of a small garden. That is a luxury reserved for extensive lay-outs where you may pass from a cultivated stretch to the contrast of a hidden corner which appears to be left to nature. In a small area a wild patch merely looks as though you have neglected to weed it.

The rough plan of the garden was already made when we bought the cottage, the limits being the walls which surrounded the small holding. It was doubly shielded on the north by the unkempt thorn hedge growing high above the wall; and a similar ancient hedge divided the garth from the garden. Doubtless we shall continue to give these names to what will really be now all cultivated. A dale garden usually means a vegetable patch, with a bias towards potatoes, and a few flowers at the edges. When we are harvesting potatoes in the strip by the road passers-by stop to ask if they are coming up well; but there is not the same interest or the joy of comparison if we happen to be digging, say, carrots or beets.

A few odd gardens such as that we pass down the moor road, a flat restful stretch closed in at the bottom by lofty trees, are given over to flowers. The mistress loves that garden, and when sometimes her family declares that it should be planted with potatoes, she insists: 'Nay, I'll keep my flowers. There's nothing to look at in a potato'; a good sentiment aesthetically, if admittedly not a patriotic one in these days. She says, and rightly we think, that potatoes would not grow under the high trees where her flowers will.

Exceptions prove the rule, and on the whole the potato garden is right because it is practical. It is what the piece of land, the garden of old surveys, was allotted for long ago when the houses were built. The narrow stone-edged bed under the house wall was often the only flower garden, and it is astonishing what flower lovers will make of this border and ensure that there is always some bloom in it.

Such a bed is the only garden in front of the cottage. It borders

The Well in the Garth

the flagged path that leads to the garth, and looks on to the cobbles which form the entrance. In the middle of the cobbles we planted a John Downie crab-apple tree to commemorate the second name of the house, 'Crabtree,' and this winter we intend to put a red hawthorn on either side of the gate.

Next summer we shall turn the garth into a lawn, or more probably, fill it with potatoes. This year it has merely been periodically scythed and had potatoes planted in one corner to clear the weeds. We shall miss the cock which resulted from each scything of the grass and which stayed in the garth until Mr. Kirkbride had time to fetch it away, and we shall miss the smell of hay from the terrace outside the garden door.

The well will be the principal feature of this part of the garden, as it was once an important factor in the life of this corner. It and a well on the green were the chief sources of water supply for the houses at Town Head. Water was first laid to the village from a spring on the opposite side of the valley, but there was rarely enough force to carry it up the hill; and the two wells continued to provide for the people until the town's supply was eventually drawn from a spring called Lanty Bog on this side. The new reservoir is on the hill just behind the cottage and occupies the site of the pinfold.

The well on the green was for general use; but, as cattle drank there, for household drinking most people brought their pails into what is now our garth. It was this custom which made Jimmy Trotter put his notice, 'Sneck gate,' for the users of the well.

'Aye, Ah 've seen manny a hundred buckets hugged fra' yon well,' Geordie tells us.

Now and again old people who have lived in the cottage at one time, or visited there, come to see us, and as they walk up the garth they almost invariably say, deliberately, as if the memory of it were just coming back: 'There used to be an old well here, didn't there?' We point it out, and they seem somehow surprised that the well has survived their going; as if they felt it as something human which must pass away with time as they must.

If the inhabitants no longer rely on the well it is invaluable to us for watering the garden. The soil is light and dry, and gardens and grass thrive in what is termed a 'droppy' season; that is when rain comes little but often. The last two years have been exceptionally dry springs which have occasioned constant watering. The water-butt soon failed us; but although we emptied the well each night it was always full again in the morning. It has never run dry within living memory or hearsay. We have planted foxgloves round it and dusky crane's-bill, ling and heather, snowdrops, wild daffodils, and forget-me-nots; later we shall carry a flower border above it.

It is not a deep well, but the outlet of a spring which rises higher up the hill-side and runs near the surface. We can hear where it enters the garth under the north wall, and after heavy rain can trace its downward course by the sound. No doubt it would be possible to open it out and have a stream running through the garden, but it is unlikely that we shall ever bring ourselves to part with the well.

One winter's morning we set to work to re-lay the paved path, which was worn and broken where it rose from the well to the end strip of garden; a troublesome task to accomplish neatly because of the slope. We removed a broken slab, and digging down came upon a larger one. Curiosity incited us to go deeper, and we discovered a third slab. Further excavations yielded no more, but the flags were useful for completing the path. Their presence seemed to imply that at two periods the garden had been at lower levels. We wonder which of our predecessors laid that first stone, and when he did it, and what he was like.

We are always told that the end strip was a lovely garden, and, although its history indicates that it has fluctuated between good and bad times, lying as it does on a southern slope, it is a piece of land which repays cultivating. When we came it had run wild for several years, and two lichen-covered gooseberry bushes, an enormous quantity of mint, and a few white daisy and montbretia plants springing up amongst the rough grass and nettles were the only indications that it had ever been anything more than the unkempt strip of land to which it had deteriorated.

Gooseberry bushes are as certain a sign of man's habitation as are nettles. Blooming alone or forming part of an old hedge they give sure proof that a house once stood near them; and a search will often reveal the line of its foundations.

The mint covered about a quarter of the ground, and was as high and rank as the grass and nettles. It still comes up like a weed, but we are gradually confining it to a mint bed.

When we came to work in the garden ourselves it was already its second season. The previous spring we had employed a man to pare off the sods and plant potatoes on most of the ground. He laid path edges with some of the quarry stones, but did not make the paths. He carried out our casual instructions in a perfunctory but quite inspired way, as if he were recovering a recollected plan rather than making a new one. During this process we discovered that the strip had been in two terraces divided across the centre by a narrow stone-edged border, and this we retained as a bed for flowers for cutting.

The potatoes thrived on the fallow land, although the plants received little attention. We earthed them up on a flying visit in a heat wave, and later gathered them with similar speed. Each root yielded a substantial pile, and the whole crop resulted in

five sackfuls from two stones of seed. Geordie wandered in and
out of the garden whilst we were turning up the roots, and watched
with a fascination which had a slight bitterness in it, because his
own potatoes were a failure that year and he had few to dig up
in the autumn.

'Ye 'll 'a' for ivver o' taties,' he said.

He ruminated for a time, and then he continued: 'Ah reckon
Ah did wrang i' putten in earlies. Ah sud 'a' putten in backerlies,
though some likes early backerlies best.'

An hour or two later he shuffled up the path again. 'They 're
cu'in' up as dry as a chip,' he remarked. 'Ye 'll be huggin' 'em
in ta morn.'

'It 's a good crop, isn't it?' we said as we dug a fresh root.

'Aye.' Then as he turned to go he repeated: 'Ye 'll 'a' for
ivver o' taties.'

The potatoes had a plentiful dressing of manure, which was
not actually necessary on land which had not recently been cultivated. The manure came at the suggestion of Manny, to whom it
is an extra profit from his horse. He stopped us one day in the
street. 'I was thinking you 'd be wanting some manure for the
garden,' he said, 'and I 've kept a load or two back in case. You
see, I haven't got a great lot, and it 's good manure, and I like to
oblige my customers.'

That autumn we filled the sheltered top half of the garden
with fruit-trees as the nucleus of an orchard. We planted them
on a bitterly cold December day, five apple and two pear trees,
three gooseberry bushes, and a row of raspberry canes. We shall
add to these this year. We first broke up the sod wall which
the labourer had reared at the sides and spread the soil level. After
digging the holes we arranged a few sods upside down in the
bottom of each to make a firm base, placed the trees on these
with their strongest roots facing west, and stamped the soil
firmly but carefully as we filled in the holes. Night had fallen,
and a severe frost was setting in when we finished. As we sat
round the fire that night a knock came to the door, and we
opened it to find two of the K. children holding a large sack of
straw in their hands. 'Father says if you don't put this round the
fruit-trees they 'll die in the frost,' they explained. We gratefully took the straw, and with the aid of a flash-light, and helped
by the two boys, spread it over the roots.

The next morning we planted the crab-apple tree. The mason removed a circle of the cobbles for us, and promised to come up later in the day and lay the edges back neatly, cobble-setting being a knack which has to be achieved by experience. We dug a deep hole which immediately filled with water. As quickly as we emptied it it refilled, and we realized that we had struck the line of one of the occasional springs that rise temporarily on the hillsides after heavy rain. The mason diverted this a little and turned it into the road drain. The tree blossomed in the spring and in October we picked seven fat red crab-apples. Esther, the little girl who brings our milk, herself a keen gardener, is very interested in our labours and particularly in the crab-tree. She used to hand the milk can in at the door, and, while it was being emptied, run to the tree to see how the fruit was growing. She received one of the seven apples. Geordie had another, and declared: 'That's not a crab. It's more like a plum.'

This was how the garden stood when we came to it at the beginning of the second season, determined to make the most of it as part of our war effort. It needed concentrated work, because of the late spring.

We made some of the paths as we went along so as to get the good top soil for the beds. This necessitated digging huge pits which we filled with stones and covered with a layer of ash. The dogs found the unexpected chasms disconcerting as they rushed along the paths whenever we went into the garden. They became so adept at avoiding them that they have never used the paths to the same extent since, but run round the wall like goats.

Day by day we forked, raked, and planted; potatoes and other roots, all the varieties of the cabbage family, salads, peas, and beans. Fanatically we worked in the long nights that the extra hours of daylight gave us until every inch was filled. Turnips and beans were squeezed between the fruit-trees; cabbages snuggled in the potato ridges; onions, part seedlings part plants, were allotted an important corner; a row of peas overhung the wall to the temptation of small passers-by. As we planted the last beds the first seeds were already sprouting.

We reserved a patch for herbs, and in our enthusiasm even made asparagus and strawberry beds. Under the wall at the top, facing full south and sheltered on the east and west, we put tomato and marrow plants. The tomatoes wilted at first with the change

from the greenhouse to our cold climate; then in the sudden
heat wave their leaves shrivelled in the hot sun. Visitors declared
that we should not get a tomato from them. In our choice of
plants, time of setting, and judgment of results, we had to keep
in mind that we were in a moorland district and 800 feet above
sea level.

As the cold weather gave way to heat still the drought persisted and made it necessary to water the garden every evening.
The onions, being near the well, received a more ample share
than the marrows, whose bed was at the farthest corner beyond the
tomatoes. Every night we filled can after can until the well was
empty save for a layer of mud on the bottom.

The soil, though stony, is dark and peaty, and engrains itself
down finger nails and works a way into any footwear. When dry
it becomes so light and fine that it is almost a necessity to press
new growth firmly into it a week or two after planting. A high
wind in a drought leaves cabbages and lettuces loose on their
stalks. But it is rich good soil.

If it grows plants well it grows weeds luxuriantly. The seeds
of millions are in it waiting to germinate as soon as they come near
enough to the surface. One day the beds are clear, the next a
green carpet. Now it is shepherd's purse, now docks, now buttercups, now crane's-bill. In three weeks they will smother any plant,
and close round a solid lettuce until the outside leaves wither.
This year's digging encouraged the growth of several varieties of
wild pansies whose seeds had not germinated the previous year.
They poked up from every bed, and in a week or two the bright
little faces of the flowers shone out so cheerily that we had not
the heart to uproot them. Forget-me-nots, too, were prolific
weeds. The horse-radish surprised us; we saw nothing of it the
first year, but when we cleared the weeds in the second season
an enormous patch came into sight.

The weeds spread to the cobbles, where they were joined by
grass and dandelions. Here also every one had an urge to uproot
them. Visitors would snatch a few as they came in or stood to
say good-bye; one friend spent hours with salt and boiling water,
and finally bought us a tin of weed killer; another suggested sheep
dip. For ourselves we have not yet decided whether it is better
to pull out the weeds and leave the loose earth ready to receive
any drifting seeds or kill them and let them show brown and dead

where they lie. In fact, we are not sure that we like the cobbles as well without them as with them.

We tried to capture to the full the joy of this first planting because never again should we have the combination of a new garden all our own and a country at war demanding that we should make full use of it A few packets of flower seeds, cornflower and marigold, godetia and larkspur, sown under the hedge have softened the severity of land given up almost entirely to vegetables; and night-scented stocks have sweetened the air with their fragrance for our nightly explorations.

Those strenuous days were relieved by the interest of the passers-by and the talks we had with them about the weather and their gardens as compared with ours. One man who has a large garden and is the acknowledged expert of the village told us that peas and carrots did well here but onions did not grow big. We proudly showed him our robust onion bed, but refrained from mentioning the failure of the broad beans. He is one of those generous fellow gardeners who pop a bundle of cabbage plants over the wall.

Sometimes on hot evenings, Geordie sat on the well on the green to catch the passers-by, and scraps of conversation were wafted easily to us because, Geordie being deaf, it is necessary for the other person to speak loudly. Mr. Brown, an old man himself, is his usual companion.

'Ah could just do to be on Redcar sands now,' he said one very close evening.

'Aye,' said Geordie, but in a tone of indifference, because he was perfectly happy sitting there in the sun.

'Ah 've been out o' England yance,' said his companion.

''Es ta?'

'Aye, to t' Isle o' Man.'

'Whya, that 's i' England.'

'Weel, it may be, but tha 's to gan ovver t' watter to 't.'

Then, after a pause: 'What does ta say, George, if tha asks for a week's holiday, and we 'll ga ti Blackpool. Tha Kate 'll gi' thee a five-pun note, weea't she?'

'An' wheear sud we gan?'

'To t' seaside, to be sure.'

Another pause, and then Geordie slowly rose. 'Whya, what sud Ah deu bi t' sea?' he said as he made for the house.

E

The Paved Courtyard

We echoed him. What would Geordie do anywhere but in the Yorkshire dales?

Another evening the subject of air raids and food was broached. 'They was bombing i' Newcastle o' Monday,' said the visitor. 'Thar's a woman staying up at our 'ouse just to get away from it a bit. They 'even't seen a hegg for weeks, and little cheese.'

'Whya, they 'll 'a' thar ration.'

'Aye; but what's two ounces? A canary 'll eat it i' one meal.'

A lorry grated up the hill with a load of lime, and the talk turned on liming activities, which have increased with the war.

'Ah think nowt o' basic slag,' said one. 'Ah yance near killed a hoss wi' it. Ah kept it too long. Nay, gi' me lime ivvery time.'

Sometimes we sat on a form, which we call the summer seat, above the fruit-trees, and looked down the village street and beyond it to where the hill of Addlebrough reared itself to guard us from the south while the sound of distant voices came gently up to us and the fragrance of night-scented stocks hung in the air. Sometimes we took our tea on to the flagged square at the west, or on to the grass in the garth from where we saw only the roofs of the village and the hills beyond; or we sat on the bink and looked westward to the upper dale. But of all our open-air eating-places the favourite was the paved courtyard at the back.

This courtyard is all that remains of the odd garden. The garage wall bounds it on the east, the kitchen wall on the south— the back door with the eternity knocker is here. The north side is a terrace with the high field wall above it; we plan to have ferns and flowers on the terrace, but at the moment it houses a load of wood stacked in Norwegian fashion. The west side is the house wall, and between its two windows we have planted an espalier Victoria plum-tree. This takes the place of the only one of the two plum-trees left when we bought the cottage. We could see by the intricate pattern of nails on the wall that it had once been a flourishing tree, but it was stunted by the time we came and had only one flowering branch high up the house side. We had to choose between it and a back door and so it had to go. Already our new one is spreading fresh shoots along the wall.

The courtyard has a slightly foreign air. We were reminded as we sat at our evening meals on the hot days of June of meals in shady places in Bavaria or Italy. It was an unusual sensation under the northern fells where summers are short and evenings chilly, so that we follow the sun instead of avoiding it. It will be something to remember in winter days as we cut a way through snow drifts banked in the yard above the kitchen door.

THE HEAT-WAVE came suddenly and caught us unawares. Bodies so recently braced to resist the cold could not adjust themselves rapidly enough to the change. Even on the moor, where, as a rule, in summer you can feel the air grow colder as you rise from the valley, it was close; we realized the abnormal state when the gamekeeper went by in his shirt sleeves, not even carrying a coat.

Geordie succumbed to the general exhaustion. One morning he, too, left his coat behind when he went up to feed his hens. After an unusually long absence which must have included many rests on the way he came trudging back over the green with a large handkerchief tucked under his hat to protect the back of his neck.

For a few days it was a damp heat which permeated the old houses until the moisture ran down the walls and rose from the floors. Open windows could not disperse it because of the absence of any breeze. People lingered outside until hours when they would usually have been in bed.

Such heat is generally a storm breeder and ends in violent thunder, which may unsettle the weather for weeks; but this year thunderstorms only cleared the air for a few hours. On the morning after one of them we met our neighbour sitting with his pail in front of him on the relic of the sandbags up the road.

'It's nice to-day,' we said.

'Aye,' he said, 'it's purer nor yesterday.'

'You don't like the heat, then?'

'Nay, Ah doa't like it like it war yesterday. Ah could stand it yance, but Ah can't now. Ah could stand it mowin', and that's not easy wark. That was afore the days of machines. We 'ed to mow an acre an' a hauf i' yar day, and Ah did it manny a time.'

He looked out along the green road, and saw himself a young man again, fit and able for a hard day's work. Then the present came back.

'Ah 'se near killed wi' me back this morning,' he said.

'Is it bad?' we asked.

'Aye, bad eneugh.'

He pulled himself to his feet. 'Ah mun get on to sarrer t' 'ens,' he said, 'or they 'll think Ah 'se not cu'in' to-day.'

The Gamekeeper

'Sarrer,' a dialect word for 'serve,' is rarely heard now.

The oppressive heat wore itself out, and gave way to summer days as perfect as we have known in the Yorkshire dales. The gardens were exotic mixtures of spring and summer. Orange tulips flaunted themselves against magenta peonies, and had scarcely faded when the lupins flowered. The lilac-trees were in full bloom, and large bunches given to us filled the house with their fragrance.

About this time we spent a day on the moors with the game-keeper. Following his slow steady stride, which covered the rough ground quickly and easily, we took the east road and turned left over the moor along Fleakstone Ridge, which dies away at the tarn. One of the reasons for our walk was to enable the game-keeper to show us where we could cut peat from a long disused pot.

To reach this we crossed a stretch of bare ground, where a few years ago a moor fire raged for days. The fire worked down to the peat and was only stopped by the digging of deep trenches round the blaze. The burning away of the peat has left a surface of gritstone and gravel which new tufts of heather, springing up from seeds blown by the wind, are now beginning to cover.

The dead body of a badger told the story of an animal which

is only a rare visitant to the moor. This one had lived alone for two years in its earth under the ridge when the gamekeeper ended its life with his gun because of the damage it was doing to the grouse, and sold the skin for making badger brushes.

Tiger, a large black setter, scented the baby grouse as they squatted almost indistinguishable in the heather, and stood untiringly with one foot poised until he was noticed. He has been a great help to the gamekeeper in ringing the young grouse in order to discover how far they eventually stray from their breeding grounds. Nothing turned him from his often self-appointed task as we crossed the moor, not even a hen bird feigning a broken wing; but when we sat down by the tarn he ceased to be a working dog and was ready for any amount of attention.

Above the tarn three curracks, Conny Tommy, Tarn Ridge, and Tarn Beacon, marked the summits of hills which on clear days give fine views of Swaledale, but that day the valley lay hidden under a summer haze. There might have been nothing in the world but moorland. The gamekeeper, knowing his ground, led us an easy way back from the tarn past a hidden spring, which the sheep know and seek out in dry weather, to a green track made as a road to old lead mines.

As we stood by the ruined blacksmith's shop, with its sleeping-place above, did we imagine the sound of voices as though a group of men were coming up the track returning from their Sunday holiday in their homes in distant villages, with wallets on their backs filled with enough food to last them the week? Was it only the wind that rustled as we peered into the room where they used to sit round the fire telling of the latest appearance of the headless black dog or the news of a traveller lost on the moor? Surely now and again the old miners gather here and talk of the good or bad veins they struck, of narrow escapes, of the lead that was so rich that when held up it shone like a looking-glass.

Below the lead mine we crossed the west moor road, and followed a green track to where a shooting hut stands with a few trees in a space walled off from the moor. The walls were built in the eighteenth century to enclose a good spring; and when the moor eventually became the property of the Crown this oasis remained with its former owners.

We gathered sticks from it and made a fire in the hut to boil the kettle for tea. In the soft drowsiness of the summer afternoon it was unutterably quiet. The sheep lay on the cropped grass in front of the hut as if they liked our presence there. A few stray cotton flowers dotting the wiry grass beyond seemed the spirits of birds which had lived among it. When we tire of human voices and human associations we think we will build a little house and go and live in that enclosure by the spring.

Whilst the moor birds were filling the hills with life the lowland birds were busy. The grass in the garth was scythed, and in a single day was made into hay and forked into a cock. News of the seeds and insects thus turned up must have been broadcast amongst the bird population, for that evening the garth was like a sanctuary. A pair of wheatears with their four fledgelings were the first arrivals; a male redstart which we had often seen in the distance flew over once or twice but did not stay; then two yellow wagtails came, and the cock bird, hopping on to the hay, preened himself luxuriously whilst the hen bird darted about the grass to gather food for the family. As soon as she had collected a beakful of insects the cock bird joined her, and together they disappeared into a meadow on the other side of the road. In a few minutes they were back, and the hen set to work again while the cock resumed his display on the hay. Time after time they returned and their behaviour was always the same.

Whilst watching the wagtails, we noticed a willow warbler disappear into the thick growth under an old privet-tree, and later we found her nest. The cone-shaped hollow lined with feathers remained safe from cats and other marauders while the eggs hatched and the fledgelings thrust hungry mouths through the narrow opening and finally grew up and left the nest. The warblers kept up a sweet refrain in the thorn hedge through the summer, and vied with the chaffinches and wagtails in filling their beaks with midges.

One of the few pleasant memories of the war will be the long, light evenings of the hot, if fleeting, summer of 1941. Whether they were good for country people is questionable; certainly no one here seemed to be in bed before midnight. We sat late on the summer seat at the top of the garden, inhaling the pungent scent of our tomato plants as we looked between the blossoming fruit-trees down the moor road. We could see, far below, the seat at the corner crowded with men and boys, whose voices carried up to us in the still air. Few made any move until the clock struck eleven, when there was a general exodus. As the last footsteps died away a deep peace settled on the valley while it still lay in daylight.

About the middle of June we went up the moor to cut our peat. This being in the nature of an experiment, and our time being limited, we only cut what amounted to eight sackfuls. We visualize a tall neat stack next year like that in the barn of the only local farmer who cuts peat on a large scale. Once we had opened out the pot, pared off the top layer of turf, and come to the soft substance, the work was not hard. Carrying it away and spreading it on the heather to dry was the most laborious part. We were glad to find a good proportion of the yellow underlayer, which dries the hardest and so lasts longest on the fire.

We hoped as we worked to find relics of the tools of past diggers buried in the peat. When the trenches were being made to stop the moor fire seven wooden spades were discovered; but these were put on one side for a few days and crumbled away. While working in his pot further west, the farmer dug up a wooden wheel from a peat cart. This consists of two solid semicircular pieces of wood pinned on to a thick centre cross-piece; in use the axle and the wheel moved round together.

No such treasures came our way, but it was pleasant there on the moor. A gentle wind blew on our faces as from above the peat pot we looked across the stretch of heather to where the lake of Semerwater lay in its encircling hills as if no valley divided it from us.

In a week's time, when the peats had hardened a little, we set them, to allow the wind and air to get to both sides. We had been rather late with the cutting, but in the heat of this year they dried long before the usual period of a month. We gathered them in the evening, and were picking up the last about eleven o'clock. The unaccustomed warmth, and the broad daylight, gave the impression of summer in more northern countries. As we stacked the peat in the yard near the wood logs we felt the satisfaction of having exercised our ancient rights of turbary. We had used the privilege expressed in the old saying: 'If you raise a reek you can gather peat.'

June is one of the easy months in dale farming. The lambs are now on the fells with their mothers, and shearing, heralding haytime, is not due until the end. It is a period when odd jobs are taken in hand. Mr. Kirkbride went up every day to mend walls;

and two farmers' sons were busy with the same work on the green lane. The snowy winter had weakened the dry walls badly and left many gaps, some large enough to require the frame to keep the line of the new piece straight.

The slack time is a favourite one for weddings. This year we had three, and the unwonted number almost went to our heads. The fact that nearly every one in the village is related to either the bride or the bridegroom makes a wedding into a large family concern.

Three men discussed one of the ceremonies on the green. Mr. Brown had stood and watched it in the heat until some butter he was carrying home 'had near run to nowt.' He opened the subject.

'Aye,' he said, 'she 's a guid looker an' a guid worker.'

'Ah reckon,' said another, 'that when a man gits a girl like yond he 's gitten a prize.'

'We sall 'a' to 'ave a bit o' wedding cake,' interrupted the youngest hopefully.

Another man coming up from the village joined the group. 'There 's a lot o' fine women an' fine dresses down yonder,' he remarked.

'Aye, an' thar 'll be plenty o' mothers' meetings to-neet,' said Mr. Brown; and they all smiled knowingly, oblivious of the fathers' meeting in which they were taking part.

Mr. Brown again turned the conversation on to weddings when he sat on the well with Geordie that night.

'I 've heard me mother tell that she rode to her wedding on a hoss, and that there was fourteen couples wedded that day. Efter t' wedding all t' men o' t' village was trottin' for ribbins—all colours, red and green and yellow. 'Es ta 'eard tell on it, George?'

'Nay,' said Geordie, 'Ah kens nowt aboot ribbins.'

'Minnd, Ah 've not seen it mesen. Ah 've just 'eard mi mother tell on 't.'

They are fast dying out themselves, those people who have

*E

heard their mothers tell of old customs. Few now remember even the tales of guests walking in couples round Muker church in Swaledale after a wedding.

The drought continued, and the farmers began to be anxious about the hay. During the long, hard winter, when extra feed was needed for the sheep, most of them had had to buy hay, and they were hoping for a heavy crop this year. Apart from the added expense, hay from the lowlands does not equal their own sweet mixed herbage. With all the moisture dried out of the shallow soil, growth stopped, and the hot sun burnt what grass there was, in places so badly that it killed the tender shoots of the fog which should follow the hay. There was doubt whether to cut and be sure of a crop of some sort, or wait a little longer on the chance of rain and risk the weather breaking altogether if it came.

Whether the crops were thin or not, June brought a special beauty to the meadows. Each evening we stood at a favourite gate and marvelled at the wealth of colour suddenly let loose in this sober land. It was never the same; every day marked an inexorable step in the progress of the year. Among the waving grasses, buttercups and daisies, bright pink clover, mauve meadow crane's-bill—this a peculiar product of dale meadows and distinct from blue crane's-bill—yellow hawkweed, reddish-brown sorrel, pink bistort, sprightly cow parsley, and innumerable other flowers were mingled. First one predominated, then another; now yellow was the leading colour, now white.

The buttercups made the bravest show. They were suddenly an unrestrained glory of gold, flaunting their colour against the background of sombre fell; then as suddenly they ceased to gild the valley, and took their place amongst the rest. The pig-nut's feathery blooms followed, until it seemed as though the meadows had been covered with foam through which the rainbow colours of the other flowers were faintly reflected.

The trees were in their rich summer splendour, except for the ashes, whose leaves, still in their young yellow freshness, were a reminder of how long spring had delayed.

Now flocks of shorn sheep were as conspicuous on the pastures as their lambs had been earlier in the year. We went up to the moor farm on the hill behind us to watch the clipping.

The big sheep-shearings, when twenty to thirty men met at one farm and finished a large flock in a day, are events of the past.

A few farmers keep up the custom of helping each other with the clipping, but small farmers have often no extra help; at the moor farm the son does all the clipping while the father fetches the sheep and folds the fleeces ready for the wool buyer. The son, having the advantage of being able to clip equally well with either hand, is able to get through the work with the minimum of movement of either himself or the sheep.

There was an air of timelessness in the scene which we watched that day; the two men moving about their tasks; the shorn sheep huddled in a corner; the cur dog waiting the command to drive them into the higher pasture; and for background the farm buildings, the barns and shippon at one end, and the house, bare of sheltering trees, opening straight on to the pasture at the other. It seemed a natural continuance of work which has altered little since sheep farming began. Wars have shaken the land, machines have replaced the craftsmen, new inventions have come quicker than we can keep pace with them, but this work has gone on unchanged under the everlasting

Mr. Brown.

hills. Milking may be done by electricity, but we are slow to relinquish clipping by hand.

The artist sketched the two men working, and whilst the father was busy with the sheep I took over his job and rolled up the fleeces. I can feel now the rough oily touch of the wool as I turned in the edges and folded the fleece so that only the clean under part showed.

'Have you found any cades?' the farmer asked with a twinkle in his eye.

'Aye,' said the son, 'there'll be onny number. There's yan on my hand now.'

'They bite,' said the farmer.

Having been warned, I found plenty of these sheep lice, but avoided being bitten. The heap of snowy fleeces grew as we talked of the 'rise,' that is the growing wool between the skin and

The Circus came to the Next Village

the matted fleece, of hogs and gimmers and shearlings, of how
you can tell the age of a sheep by the number of its teeth. Then
lambs and sheep were marked with a cross and a letter B in tar;
and the day's work was done.

June brought its entertainments. There were the dialect
plays, written, produced, and performed by dalespeople in a village
lower down the valley. This annual performance, now becoming
a part of the local life, brings an air of festival.

Then the circus came to the next village, and caused much
excitement because circuses are not common in these parts now.
We owed its visit to the fact that many of the coast resorts were
barred. The little company, headed by a member of the Sanger
family, journeying slowly to the north-west corner of Scotland,
can seldom on their tour have had so lovely a site as this village
green under the Wensleydale fells. The artist painted the circus
from a raised corner where she could look down on to the faded
pink-and-yellow-striped marquee and the old buses and tents
which were the dressing-rooms and sleeping quarters of the
company. Presently she was joined by a small red-haired Scots
boy who wanted to buy the picture for two shillings to take back
to his grandmother with whom he lived in Glasgow. He was
anxious for his father and mother, who were the clown and a singer
in the circus, and as many of the other members as possible, to be in
the picture, and at various times he brought them all out
to pose.

In the end Mr. Sanger bought the picture; and we followed the circus to nearby places to paint more. We quickly developed a personal feeling for the striped marquee; for the performing dogs, Jolly, Rio, Pat, Terry, Fellow; for Barney the donkey; and for the two Shetland ponies, Aber who danced, and Deen who skipped, and whose names together spelt Aberdeen, in which town they were bought. We came to respect the quiet of the afternoon when the whole company tried to snatch a little sleep.

There was the lady who helped her husband, the conjurer, in the ring, and at the back was incessantly collecting props and packing away those already used. And the acrobatic family—the young trapeze artiste, the mother who worked with her, and the father who had had to come back to the trapeze when his son joined the army. There was a comradeship about them all which must have helped in the smooth running of this hippodrome circus.

Two days ahead were all that Mr. Sanger felt that he dared arrange in a war. In their moving life food restrictions also created difficulties. 'Food!' said Mrs. Sanger, who managed the performing dogs. 'I stood in a queue three-quarters of an hour this morning. It was one of those farm carts come in from the country. I could see two chickens, and I looked at them, and wondered if they would last until my turn came. A lady behind me said: "Do you think that one will be expensive?" I said I didn't know; but what I did know was that my turn came first. Well, I got them, and I expect they 'll be as tough as Old Nick, and I 'll have to boil them three or four hours.'

Whilst the artist painted the circus from all angles I joined in the life behind the scenes. 'Nice weather for travelling,' the man who had come for the ground fees remarked pleasantly to me at the last town in which we met. 'Very nice,' I said, and felt to be a part of the circus to which we were saying good-bye, of that strange company gathered closely together for the summer months, and parting to go their separate ways, never to meet in just that combination again.

It is unwise to look too far in the future in a war; perhaps Mr. Sanger's two days ahead are best, but we cherish the hope of travelling further with the circus in happier days.

Hay-time

THE CUTTING OF Mire Land meadow opened the hay season for us at Town Head. Our neighbour told us the news over the garden wall. It excited him more than any event in the year. The following afternoon, chancing to be looking out of the east window, we saw him go through the stile by the garage and climb up the field path, a way we had never before known him take. He went up the first pasture, through the second stile, diverged a little from the path, and walked half-way across the next pasture. Here he stood and, shading his eyes, looked down to the valley. By doing so he could just see how the haymaking in Mire Land meadow was proceeding.

Immediately it was a world of hay. Once a farmer had taken the plunge the rest followed. Except on the high farms the crop would spoil if it was not cut now. We gazed on hay in all its stages; we smelt its fresh scent; the sound of mowing machines and the voices of haymakers filled our ears. This was the concentrated fever of all the harvests of lowland regions, the clover, the grass, the corn, the roots, rolled into one. It was the culmination of the year's work, the winter 'mucking,' the spreading of lime, the storing of ham and food for the workers, the engaging of hay-time men. To get the dried grass safely into the barns, to ensure the supply which was to feed the stock through the winter, was the chief concern.

It was all over so quickly. 'It maks itsel'. Thar 's neea wark wi' it,' an old farmer declared, and recollected years when the grass lay on the ground for weeks and needed constant turning. To watch the process on Croft Hill, towards which the cottage faces, was like seeing it on a cinema film. The mowing was started one evening, and created an unusual stir. It was as if Croft Hill marked the climax of haymaking. Every farmer, every man, coming down the moor road stood at a convenient gateway to gaze; some climbed on to the green for a better view, and joined other spectators on the seat.

''E 's a good hand at mowin' now, is Will.'

'Aye, 'e 's gitten one o' t' best i' t' dale.'

The reaper broke down that night, but was working again early next morning. A day's quiet while the sun dried the already baked grass, and then the meadow burst into frenzied life. Four women raking the hay into rows moved as one person at a pace which never slackened. Men following them pulled the rows into small cocks sometimes called 'jockeys.' These were forked into pikes which at night, as more help arrived, were led on sledges to the barn. The work advanced so rapidly and mechanically as to remind us of modern factories where one process follows another in quick succession to achieve the finished article.

The droughty season was the subject of continual comment on the seat at the foot of the moor road. In the fever of work only the old men had time to sit there; and it was of droughts long ago that they talked, of seasons ending in record time.

In order that the children may help with the hay the school holidays begin earlier than in the towns, a necessary arrangement because the attendance falls off as soon as hay-time begins. Both boys and girls take naturally to haymaking and enjoy it, for the country child accepts work as a recreation much more readily than the town child. Helping on the farm, delivering milk, carrying parcels, running errands, are jobs done cheerfully and as a matter of course.

At the sawmill where the electricity used to be made a good trade is done in hay rakes. The ash poles stored in the outside sheds, the curved pieces for the bows, and the teeth, which had been turned by the power of the water-wheel, had been fitted together during the preceding weeks. Every year several children's rakes are made and find a ready sale.

The favourite job with the children is to sit astride the horse and drive it and the sledge to and from the barn. Esther was particularly clever at this, and brought her loads through a gateway, along a narrow lane, across the moor road, and through another gateway to the barn without any mishap.

The children's help has been specially valuable this year when labour is short, and would have been more so had not the weather itself proved so great a helper. Only a few Irishmen in place of the usual crowds waited to be hired for the hay season this year. The farm below us employed two men from the Yorkshire Wolds, one who had been there during the 1914–18 war, and the other a new-comer. Both were able to work long hours without tiring, and they dealt with the job in hand, whether it was scything, strewing, loading, or forking, with ease and assurance. The last meadow was cleared on the day they were due to leave. Only one or two sledge loads remained when they were obliged to stop to catch their train at four o'clock. They returned to their homes in time for the great corn harvest on the Wolds.

'We've had a reet good time,' they said, 'and we'll be back again another year. It's a grand piece of country, this, and we hope we've not seen the last of it.'

Hay-time ended suddenly, except on a few high farms where some acres lingered into the unsettled August days. The fields were bare and silent. Barns exuded the smell of new hay. Everywhere there was the satisfaction of another harvest safely accomplished.

Amid the rush the regular work went on; cows had to be milked, and on the isolated farms the milk made into cheese, neither of which jobs will wait. Even before the war farm-houses at which cheese was made were becoming rare and their number has since been halved. The few farms which are still allowed to make it because the lack of a roadway renders the collection of liquid milk difficult must send their product to join the government stock.

We called at the by-side farm one day when they were making cheese. The mistress had just poured the new milk through the strainer and was putting in the rennet when we arrived. A few weeks ago we were presented with an addition to our collection of bygones, a rack which supported the sieve for straining the milk, 'a brig for t' sile' it is called locally. In shape it is not unlike the racks which are rested across baths to hold sponges.

We watched the curds being broken up and put into a mould, the 'chesford,' ready for the press. An iron press is used now, but an old stone one remains in the outbuilding. This is a cumbersome contrivance with a large square stone block hanging from a wooden frame in which it was screwed up and down to release or exert the pressure. Many stones from old cheese-presses are built into walls. We have part of one in the wall by the garden door, and we use a flat base which we found in the lean-to as a flagstone.

The previous day's cheese was put into brine for three days before it joined the others on the shelf. It is this pickling in brine which makes the farm-house cheeses superior to dairy ones. Both, of course, benefit from the sweetness of the pastures which give its particular flavour to Wensleydale cheese so that it is never the same when made in other districts.

The mistress enjoys cheesemaking, as she enjoys many jobs on the farm, where she has even helped with clipping sheep as the women did in olden times. Hers is a necessary attitude for a full and happy life on a hill farm.

One Sunday evening, as we came down the road from the moor, we noticed an unusual number of people standing at the doors or moving on from one little group to another in the main street. When the milk was delivered we heard that the Home Guard had been called out, some from church, to look for parachutists who were reported to have been seen to drop from an aeroplane. Long before it was discovered, two days later, that what had resembled parachutes were smoke bombs from a British plane, the tension had relaxed.

Not that we are easily alarmed. We take our bombs calmly, while never ceasing to wonder why it should be considered worth while to waste any on us. Except for one occasion when several windows were broken, a fire was started, and one sheep killed, in a nearby village, which now speaks importantly of its blitz, the bombs have only succeeded in making craters on the moors and upper pastures. We are rather proud of our craters, but realize that if one had been made, say, on our little green there would not have been much of us left. After the largest bomb fell, a visitor from a town insisted on going home early the next day to the safety of shelters.

We almost lived on salads from the garden now, radishes,

cress, and crisp solid lettuces; and we began to pick our early
peas. The asparagus, after delaying many weeks, thrust its
feathery spikes through the dry ground. We thinned the apples
which had formed on the new fruit-trees.

The mushrooms were a help to the larder. Our occasional
walks usually yielded a pocketful, but never a large amount; the
Kirkbride children, out in the fields at dawn, were too near for
that. People came along the roads with bulging pockets or bags
and a self-conscious air. The mushrooms were chiefly white
button ones which grew equally well among the fog in the meadows
or on the pastures; we even picked them on the grassy edges of
the road over the moor.

A friend sent us up some crayfish which he had caught in the
river. We ate the claws and tails of these lobster-like creatures;
and thought them particularly delicious when they came from our
own river. The crayfish were caught by being gathered into nets
as they swarmed for the bait, which was rabbit guts hung on
sticks. We had never time to go fishing ourselves, but one evening as we walked by the river we saw the brown muddy little
creatures, looking very drab when compared with the brilliant
red into which they turn when boiled. Whilst we were watching
them a kingfisher, the first we had seen that year, flashed by with
the tones of the trees and the brilliant summer sky mingled in
his plumage.

I suppose that in no time in its history has this or any other
dale village had so many visitors as in 1941, for the valley provided a comparatively safe and not too distant holiday ground.
Most of them loved it; but as the season advanced there were some
who wandered about aimlessly, as if they missed the sea and a
lively beach.

Chintah's mother and aunt came this month. They had
accomplished the journey from the south coast by lifts in cars,
the last of which had brought them to our village. Learning that
we lived here, they knocked at the door about nine o'clock, not
knowing how far they were from their destination. After they
had had some supper we sat round the fire while the mother told
of her life with a musical set in Vienna and other foreign capitals,
and of that tragic parting with Chintah's father, he destined for a
concentration camp and she for safety in England. Their story
sounded strange and exotic in the quiet of a dale cottage. But

still stranger was it to hear of their life on the farm, of rising at five o'clock in the morning and tramping miles to work, never really feeling awake before they arrived; of a morning's hoeing in the fields, a quick lunch, a snatched half-hour of sleep, and work again; of farm men talking to them in their slow Sussex voices of the 'wonnerful ole horse' and the 'wonnerful ole cart.'

At the end of the week the cosmopolitan pair returned, and Chintah went on playing with the village children. 'I 'll come back to you some time, mother, when the war 's over,' she said as she waved good-bye. Before then she is to experience a nursery school run for evacuated children by the Society of Friends. We know that when we take her there she will say, in her determined voice: 'We 're not going to live in this house.' And a few weeks later we shall find her entranced with the company of other children.

It was in July that Geordie's wife died. We went to the service in the little chapel down the moor road, and afterwards watched the funeral procession, led by the coffin on a bier, wend its way slowly down the main street. It was taking to her last resting-place one of the best types of daleswomen, spare and hard-working, full of kindly thoughts and deeds. The last message she sent down to us when she felt too ill to see us was: 'Tell them I like to see them about.' We would say to her, wherever she is now: 'We miss your gentle presence on the green.'

About the middle of July a family of potters camped at the side of the road above the water-splash. The women going from house to house selling aprons and drapery first announced their presence. They were a good-looking family of mother and father, three sons, and four daughters, who somehow managed to squeeze into two tents, the smaller of which was referred to as the 'accommodation.' The camp also included four horses, one a piebald which was always called Baldy, though its real name was Tulip, and a puppy dog. Presumably the men made a living by selling horses; but during the time they were here they only seemed to stop playing cards in order to eat and sleep. Their voices rose excitedly at times, but otherwise they played quite amicably with no pause between the games. The family were on their way back to the town in which they lived during the winter to pick up their caravan ready for the autumn fairs.

They and some cousins who had camped on the high green

road in June were the sole survivals this year of the old Hill Fair. The potter woman remembered when both green roads were packed with tents and caravans for the event. Most of them stayed a fortnight; now the policeman moves them on after one night.

We were reminded of one of Geordie's descriptions of the Fair. 'Ah minnd when t' Straits Lane war packed wi' gipsies. Thar 'd be stalls wi' sweets and about thirty drinking tents, and it lasted tweea days. Aye, it war a grand day for t' young folk. It war a young folks' fair, Ah reckon. T' Fair 'Ill ud be so thick wi' couples sittin' on t' hill-side, yer couldn't finnd a way through 'em.'

Fair or no fair, the potters made an attractive picture in the camp by the road-side, and the artist spent most of a day with them. The family lined up in a row to say good-bye when we left.

'Do you ever go to Brough Hill Fair?' we asked.

'Never misses it,' said the potter woman.

'Well, perhaps we shall see you there and paint another picture,' we said.

'Yes, look out for us. You 'll find us all together. You know what I mean; we sit round our own camp fire.'

'Come and speak to us,' said the father. 'I 'm not a good kenner of faces, but just say you come from Wensleydale.'

Next morning they were gone. For a day or two they had filled the road with life, and they vanished, leaving only a heap of ashes behind them. Strange vagrant creatures they were, gathering fuel from the countryside, leading their horses to graze, cooking concoctions over the wood fire. They seemed to have cast away responsibility, and to touch only the fringe of life. When at night they heard aeroplanes overhead they remembered the washing hung over the walls and ran to gather it in, but even in this they had only themselves to consider. Yet if they came no more we should miss the picturesque camps by the roads and the friendly dignity of the occupants.

We thought of the hard-working circus people who were also summer wanderers on the roads. 'Have you the time, dear?' the potter people usually ask when you pass their camp. But the circus artiste must know the time himself. He serves an audience.

The Potters made an Attractive Picture by the Road-side

THE DULL DAYS of August came as a relief. It was refreshing to feel the rain on our faces again; to see storms sweeping down the valley; to find the hills now outlined against an angry sky, half gold half grey, now lit in sunshine, now alive with shadows of racing clouds. The invigorating air was what one expected in the dales.

The visitors were at their climax. Every house catering for them was packed, and had turned many away. Early one morning we were awakened by a knock on the door, and the artist looked out of her window to see a young man standing on the flags holding a book in his hand.

'Would it be too much to ask you to sign this for me?' he asked.

'Not at all,' she said in a sleepy voice, 'if you don't mind waiting out there for a few minutes.'

'Well,' he replied, 'I shall have to ask you to be quick because I'm catching the early train.'

We signed the book, and later learnt that the visitor had put off buying it until his last day when he could be sure that he was leaving himself with enough money to get home.

We had our personal share of visitors. Relations, friends, acquaintances, strangers, all links with the outer world, came in at our door, and we enjoyed them all. Only when they adopted what we call the 'country cottage' attitude, with its idea of playing at living and avoiding responsibility, did we object.

A few shivered in the sudden cold, and thought that we must always have that kind of weather. But, as if to contradict them, in between the dull days there came occasional perfect ones when the valley danced in the brilliance and the hills sank into tranquillity again.

On such a day while walking into the next valley we came upon the thatched barn. The air sparkled as we went up the moor, and time seemed to halt to hold the glory of summer. A pair of curlews soaring above mocked in their lofty flight the clumsy grouse; but the heather in bloom and the dwindling number of the birds warned us that autumn was at our heels. At the tarn the dunlin stood motionless in the shallow water amongst the reeds, and a few mallards flew leisurely overhead, but two stragglers were all that remained of the noisy gulls. They looked forlorn without their companions, and less striking now that they had shed their black hoods.

Beyond the tarn we dropped down into a hollow between the fells, called Bloody Vale, where legend says a fight took place between dalesmen and Scots raiders. The head of the valley into which this opens took its name, Summerlodge, from the summer pasture farms in it. The Norse settlers who founded these must at times have almost forgotten that they were not in their native land, so like is this region to the wooded hill-sides which run down to Norwegian fjords.

Where the grassy hillocks descended abruptly to a strip of ancient forest near a beck we caught sight of the barn, a long building with a steeply pitched roof outlined against the trees in the westering sun. In the interior, where the narrow light slits were widely splayed, shafts of sunlight streaming through them illuminated patches of stonework on the northern wall; streaks of light also penetrated the roof where the thatch was wearing thin. Slender beams supported the thatch; and a shallow manger with a rack above it ran round the walls. Seen down its entire length it gave the impression of an aisle in an ancient church.

Later the farmer told us that the barn was known as the hog house, and that it was used to fodder hogs and gimmer lambs in the winter; the young lambs first learn to eat hay in it. It was rethatched when he came to the farm twenty-eight years ago; but the man who did the work is dead, and now it will be difficult to find any one to undertake even the repairing of it. Thatching with ling is more trying work than thatching with straw, because the ling is harsher to handle; it is a craft in itself.

Although ling thatching was once a common roofing for barns and cottages, a few examples on derelict buildings, and one or two on inhabited houses kept up as a whim on the part of the owner, are all that remain. We are told that the tumbledown building in front of Coleshouse was one of the last in the village to retain its thatch. Although this particular use of local material to be had for the gathering has died out, ling still fills some domestic needs. It makes excellent kindling; the gamekeeper regularly brings an armful down from the moor. A bunch of it is more often used to clean the chimneys of soot than a sweep's brush, though for this purpose it vies in popularity with a gooseberry branch.

The parsley was now a green curly row. We were eating our peas and beans, and we had tried the first potatoes. No vegetables can rival those first potatoes scraped immediately after they are dug, with the earthy taste strong in them. The marrows grew almost visibly; and the onions rose out of the ground in fine globes which passers-by looked over the wall to admire.

This year has seen new landmarks dotting the valley in the silos, varying from large concrete buildings to small ones made of corrugated iron sheeting. Now the time had come for the produce of the newly ploughed fields to be loaded into them. The filling of that by the sawmill caused the greatest interest owing to its position near the road allowing one and all to stand and watch the proceedings. The North Riding machine chuffed away as it chopped the greenery forked into it, and shot it through a wide pipe into the silo. It was a mixed salad composed of fog from a meadow whose first crop had been reaped early, and an assortment of tares, peas, beans, and kale. The children, and many grown-ups too, pulled the stumpy pods from the pea straw, and shelled and ate them as they watched.

The farmer, standing in the silo, trampled down the green as it was blown in, and watered each layer with diluted molasses. As he worked on his platform far above us, silhouetted against the stone building, he seemed the personification of a new idea and all its possibilities. The load was kept convex to prevent the mixture from becoming hollow in the middle as it settled, and so decaying; several additions had later to be made at intervals to replace the sinking before it was ready for its top covering of rushes. It reminded us of the French beans which we were salting for the winter, and which settled with standing so that we had not filled our stone jar to the brim by the time the early frost cut off the supply.

The school holidays ended in August, and the dale went back to autumn work. Mr. Brown, stopping to talk as he passed the garden, was reminded of his own schooldays.

'I was born at Twaite i' Swaledale,' he said, 'and I walked to t' Keld to scule ivvery day. I' them days thar war a boggle at ivvery corner. Yar neet we thowt 'e 'd gitten us. Thar war a girt rattlin' o' cheeans, an' we childer ran for oor lives; an' in a minute tweea tups tied togither cam' blatherin' past.'

The schoolmaster, who had a long white beard, was always known as Simy Dode. He lived in a hamlet in a house called 'Up t' Steps,' and used to ride to the school every day on a white pony. When the pony needed shoeing the children all had a day's holiday.

'I had to stay i' Keld all day,' said Mr. Brown, 'and I left my food wi' Neddy Dick.'

We can imagine the child looking forward eagerly to meals with the old man, for Neddy Dick was famous all over the dale in those days because of the 'stone piano' which he had made with boulders picked from the river bed. A photograph which we were recently given of him shows an alert old man playing another of his musical instruments, a harmonium with bells fixed over it. He collected the bells up and down the dale; if the note of the chime of a grandfather's clock was one that he lacked he would worry the owner until he let him have the bell.

About this time we added a backstone pan to our collection This is a flat, round iron plate which was hung from the reckon over the peat fire, and used to bake oatcakes, havercakes in dale language. We have also been promised a cake stool, or three-leg, a wooden article rather like a small easel. When the havercake was baked underneath, it was lifted off the backstone and propped up on the pegs of the cake stool to harden in front of the fire.

Near the beginning of September we made a pilgrimage to the dale head, to follow the road which we always call Lady Anne's, because that dauntless lady took this way as she journeyed from her Yorkshire to her Westmorland castles. We like to follow Lady Anne Clifford's journeys occasionally, if only to marvel at the roads she braved with a coach and four and an enormous retinue. She tells of many overturnings of the coach, which 'we set right again, and went on.' It would seem well in this time of war and the hard days of peace which will follow for Englishwomen to be reminded of the courage and ingenuity displayed by their countrywomen in the past, for even now some vestige of the Victorian tradition that women should be sheltered and looked after persists. Women left to carry on and manage alone may be encouraged to know how a woman did it long ago, and found zest in the doing.

The new road up the valley has been made since Lady Anne's day, and, except on the level top, her route is fast losing any

semblance of a road. Only the fine grass on the ridge tells of
a firm under-surface. We passed the weather-beaten cluster of
buildings which used to be an inn called High Dyke; eerie places,
haunted not so much by any particular ghost as by some sensation left behind by the hundreds who stopped here on their
journeys, gossiped for a time, and then proceeded on their way.
We entered one of the bare echoing barns to find the earth floor
covered with toadstools. Silent and mysterious on their tall
stalks, their pale umbrella heads lined with delicate grey, they
seemed memorials of those long dead crowds whose voices had
sounded within the walls when they brought their horses for
shelter.

Past Highway House and High Hall, Wild Boar Fell with its
grand contours faced us, a giant gatepost marking the entrance
not only into another county but into a totally different one; a
soft luxuriant land with waving cornfields, hedges instead of
walls, and gracious houses on which time has laid a mellowing
hand. A mile or two further, and Lady Anne with her retinue
would be at her castle of Pendragon in Westmorland.

But we were on this side of the gateway, looking over a region
whose decay seemed as irrevocable as that of most of the castles
which Lady Anne journeyed to and rebuilt. So many reasons
have made for its decline that it seems as though nothing could
stop it; the throwing together of several small farms; the
distance, owing to the disuse of the old road, from a modern
highway. When all roads were rough this did not seem for-
midable; but people now refuse to live on the isolated sites.
Perhaps they have had their day. And yet, who knows? War
has given an added value to hill pastures, and that value must
not be let go.

It would have been good to be on the road on the last day of
September when crowds were tramping along it to the last horse
and cattle fair of the season at Brough, in Westmorland, that fair
which the potters never miss. More people came that way then
than the inn could cater for, and the farmers' wives used to set up
stalls along the road and sell refreshments to the travellers. But
when later we journeyed to the fair we did so along the valley road.

In the meantime the first tomato ripened, and autumn flowers
were gay in the gardens. Our small neighbour, Mary, came up
with a bunch of Michaelmas daisies, flowers which in themselves

seem to express the harvest. We sent some of our garden produce to the harvest festival at the church.

So we came to the last day of the month, and Brough Hill Fair. Sometimes we try to analyse our feelings about this event, to discover what makes its fascination, and why it is that something seems missing in a year that does not include a visit to it. Old people tell of bigger crowds and many more caravans and horses, and infer that we who only see Brough Hill to-day have missed its full glory. We agree that it must have been an inspiring sight, and much more picturesque when all the caravans were horse-drawn, but we cannot bring back those days. It is enough that Brough Hill is still a stirring sight, perhaps more fantastic and contradictory now that petrol-driven vehicles form so great a part of it.

If its merchandise no longer includes cattle it is still a large horse fair, and in consequence a meeting-place for farmers, gipsies, and potters. That alone is a strange combination, the farmer tied to the acres from which his living comes, and the vagrant company which does its bargaining in hundreds of English villages and towns.

This being the last fair of the season, for weeks the campers have been gradually verging from all directions to its centre, where they meet and mingle for a few days, and then have done with tents and camps and fairs until the spring. North, south, east, and west they go from here, and are swallowed up in towns for the winter hibernation.

This year we caught sight of the camp whilst we were still a mile or two away. In its rural setting under the Westmorland fells it was like a mirage, an illusion of the eye which would vanish as we looked. But the picture persisted, and soon we joined along the road crowds of people, farmers' families, young folks from the market towns, on their way to that encampment which had sprung up in a night.

We entered from the Warcop side, as the old visitors from the dales would do, and at the gate paid twopence for each wheel of our car. The long field sloping up from the entrance was lined and dotted with caravans and tents; small bowed accommodation tents, large square tents with pinnacled corners which might have been those of eastern nomads; covered carts, gaily painted gipsy caravans, luxurious modern trailer caravans. They were grouped irregularly on either side of a wide passage left for the traffic; each of the wood fires burning outside them, with a pan or kettle hung from the iron stand, the 'chitty balk,' formed a focus for a group of potter women and gaily dressed girls and children.

The professional fortune tellers' caravans with curtains drawn mysteriously across the windows were light-coloured and gaudy; and their occupants stood alluringly at the doors, beckoning as gipsies have done since centuries ago they found that they could make profit out of man's curiosity to know the future.

'Come and see what the cards say, love.   You 've got a lucky face.'

'You 'll go far, my dear.   You like to hold your head high in the world.   Come and let me see your hand.'

'I 'd like to read your fortune, dear.   I could tell you something for your good.'

There was also a subtle attraction about the low tents with swarthy figures motioning from their dim interiors.

These are the real gipsies, distinct from the potters.   This year we missed the family from the Border, the winter home of many Romanies.

The main road to Scotland which runs along one side of the pasture was lined with cars and buses.   The cheapjacks had their stalls near this entrance; the patent-medicine seller, a sweet stall around which a queue immediately formed, a game of chance, and, a sign of the times, a countrywoman selling pears and apples.

We were delighted to find again the children's roundabout. Its owner's affairs seemed to be prospering with the scarcity of petrol, for he was now employing a younger man to turn the roundabout while he sold cheap toys, string balls, and little canes, as fast as he could unpack them and place them on a ground-sheet.

The farmers congregated at the top end of the pasture, where the potters raced the horses up and down to display them at such a speed that hooves drummed upon the ground as they galloped. Here some hard bargaining was going on between a Swaledale man who had a two-year-old galloway to sell and a wiry little gipsy with skin like leather.

'Come on, now,' said the gipsy, 'sell it.'

'Nay,' said the farmer, 'tha 's not shapin' to buy.'

The gipsy examined its points again, and then he smacked the farmer's hand to indicate another bid.

Some Hard Bargaining was going on

'Come on, and I'll meet you with a pound. And you get your money. I'm well known.' He looked round challengingly at the crowd, who murmured assent.

'It's a good lile 'oss,' said the farmer.

'I know it's a good 'oss or I wouldn't be wanting to buy it. Well, another ten bob. It's my last bid,' and he smacked the farmer's hand again. 'I'm wanting to buy it because I know as soon as I've turned my back someone'll be offering you what I have. They know I'm a judge of 'osses.'

The farmer shook his head.

'I'm buying it in the air as you might say. I'm not asking for its pedigree or whether it's got any vices. I'm just taking it, same as I would a wife. It'll have a good home.'

'It's a good heeame whar it is. Ah'se not set on selling it. Ah'se fond o' t' lile 'oss.'

'Well, I'm going,' said the gipsy. 'I'll give you what I said last at the gate as you go out.' As he walked swiftly away three men immediately offered the same price for the horse, but the farmer shook his head and moved into the throng.

It was strange to see the potters who had camped on the moor road in the crowded company.

'Fair times are so busy that you haven't got time for anything,' said the mother.

The 'accommodation' was there, but now they had the caravan

also and were anxious to show us inside.   We sat on the padded
seat opposite the miniature fire-grate with its mantel-shelf
decorated with showy ornaments, and from that point of vantage
saw the fair from a different angle.   For a few minutes we were
no longer spectators, but a part of the wandering community
whose summers are a continual flitting from place to place and
whose tradition goes back to the beginnings of history.

In the first year of the war there was no fair at Brough Hill,
although a few families pitched in the pasture for the night; but
on an appeal being sent to the authorities it was allowed to assemble
again in 1940.   Under war conditions it could not be what it was;
for one thing there was not petrol enough to run many of the handsome caravans; but there was no air of decay about it in 1941.
We were reminded of the war when we walked on corn stubble
instead of springy turf, and regulations decreed that all fires and
lights must be out by eight o'clock; but such passing inconveniences
could not kill a fair which had met here since 1331.

We thought of a happier year at Brough Hill when dusk was
falling and the crowds had gone.   Lights shone in the caravan
windows; but it was a mild evening, and many groups still sat
round the glowing camp fires, men and women smoking pipes.
Voices were low in the gathering darkness.   We felt the antiquity
of it all.   Thus for six hundred years had a community gathered
here as September gave way to October to buy and sell stock
bred on the fells.

So WE ARRIVE at that wild October evening which first started us on the story of the cottage. When the rain ceased, with the month only half gone, came a sudden sharp frost; snowstorms swept down the valley; and the hills were capped with white for several days. Winter seemed to be upon us two months early.

'You won't be stirrin' far afield to-day,' said Mr. Gill when we went down to the village.

But autumn roused itself in time. October flared forth in all her glory, and showed us that at its best it is one of the loveliest times of the year in hill country. For a period the landscape seen through a filmy haze took on a familiar yet enchanted beauty. One morning during that time a streak of sunlight piercing the mist turned the barn on Croft Hill into a cinnamon house, and transformed the sycamore beside it into a tree of gold. A curlew calling a mournful farewell made a last flight across the valley. Cobwebs spangled with moisture made networks over the thorn hedge.

Then for days the air was so clear and pure that through the morning every detail showed on Crag and Wether Fell, every wall and barn and little patch of trees, until the sun veering round in the sky threw them into shadow. Those shadowed hills were effects which only autumn could have produced; their tones were intenser than when summer veiled them in heat. As the sunset flooded the sky with colour they reflected true purple, deep bold blue, or rich dark brown. The sunsets were now more directly opposite the windows, and their pageantry might have been displayed particularly for us; for though the sun still had warmth each day it was lower in the sky. It caught the cottage windows sooner in the morning, and poured through them for most of the day.

The early frost was unusually severe.   It left a layer of ice on the water in the cans by the well.   The marrow and kidney bean plants turned black in a single night.   We hurried to cut the one remaining marrow, the largest, which weighed seventeen and a half pounds; and to harvest the tomatoes, whose yield of twenty-three pounds we felt was creditable in this upland country.   As the bulk of these were green when we picked them, we put the larger ones, wrapped in paper, in boxes to ripen, and the smaller ones we made into green tomato chutney.

As soon as the ground was dry enough we dug the potatoes, and these, though not so prolific as the year before, were a satisfactory crop.   After forking up the onions we set them out in the sun daily to dry off, and finally slung them on a piece of netting under the roof of the tool-shed.   We stored the beet and carrots, but the turnips could be left conveniently in the ground. The sprouts, curly broccoli, and savoys were green and vigorous. We burnt the refuse on a bare patch, and watched the smoke curl into the sky; but this year the satisfying garden rite was robbed of half its joy, for by the time the fire had a steadily glowing heart it had to be stamped out as darkness fell.

It was not given us to harvest our apples, except for two bakers and one small eater.   The few we had allowed to remain on the trees grew into fine specimens; but just before they were ready for picking we went out to tea, and returned to find them gone, and a next year's fruiting branch broken off a Lane's Prince Albert.

We knew that others had suffered in this way; but, with the species of optimism which has brought so many European countries to their ruin, we thought that it would not happen to us. John Burroughs says: 'The boy is indeed the true apple-eater, and is not to be questioned how he came by the fruit with which his pockets are filled.'   Whilst sympathizing with that sentiment, the future, for which we planned a more ambitious orchard, had to be considered.   Taking with us a nibbled apple which we found thrown among the cabbages, we challenged the boys who were playing marbles at the foot of the road.   We were very stern, although privately we found the meeting amusing.   Perhaps to appreciate it fully one must be familiar with the mingled charm and devilment of the small boys of the village.

'Look at that,' we said, showing them the nibbled apple, just wasted. It can't be used for anything.'

Elizabeth, the youngest child and the only girl amongst them, broke the strained silence. 'It might go in a pie,' she suggested.

'Apples are worth a lot of money in wartime,' one boy remarked.

'Aye,' said another, 'and you can be summoned for taking 'em.'

'You can,' we said, grimly, 'in wartime and ordinary times too.'

As we turned to go the smallest boy said, hopefully: 'The evacuees steal apples.'

It seemed useless to leave the matter there, anger alone being a destructive not a constructive medium. We thought of those Norwegian orchards open to the road, and wondered if a personal possession showed the value of a similar one to others. A solution seems to lie along the lines of letting the children have apple-trees themselves, and know the joys and sorrows of ownership; and this is going to be tried.

Now there came the flood of autumn sales in the market town where the farmers reap the big financial result of the year's labour. Cattle sales, bull fairs, lamb sales, tup fairs, followed each other. There was no grumbling at poor prices this year; in fact, prices were mentioned with bated breath.

'Sixty pounds bid for a cow that wouldn't have fetched twenty-eight pounds a year back,' said Mrs. Gill at the shop.

Lambs were making an average of £2 each; but the climax came when a Swaledale tup fetched 125 guineas.

The cattle vans were in use from early morning until late at night; we heard the shouts as stock from a distance was unloaded in the darkness, unaided now by lanterns. The small field opposite the green had constantly changing tenants in sheep or cattle bought by our friend the dealer at one sale and pastured there until the next. Our track over the green made a convenient turning-place for the lorry which brought them and carried them away.

The farmer from the by-side farm took a flock of draught ewes, a mixed lot, a few belonging to one man and a few to another, to one of the later sales by road. It was raining hard when we saw him the previous day.

F

'Ah 'se hoping the rain 'll stop afore neet,' he said, 'or t' becks 'll be seea full that the sheep 'll refuse 'em, an' Ah 'll 'a' to gan by t' main road.'

It cleared sufficiently to allow him to follow the old drovers' road which fords the becks on the hill-side. It is a nearer and an easier way for the sheep, and avoids the traffic of the main road up the valley. But this was an exception; the bulk of the stock was carried speedily along the modern highways.

That was the important traffic; but a constant stream of another kind coming down the moor road was a reflection of the time of the year. Horse-drawn carts brought down the harvest of the moors and woods for the thrifty farmers; loads of bracken for bedding; or rushes, which this year were also used for thatching the silos. A cart passing with bales of fleeces on its way to the station brought up the rearguard.

Calling on our friends at the by-side farm we found them just returned from an afternoon's sticking in the wooded gill. The farmer was untying the ropes which secured a neat load of kindling on the sledge. 'It was lovely up in the woods this afternoon,' his wife said, 'like a picnic.'

We received and stacked another load of logs from Raydale. There was a finality about those last additions to the autumn store; each marked a stage in the closing in of the valley for winter. This starts almost imperceptibly, but yet starts, as early as August, and by the end of October it is complete. Doors are closed, and people stay inside. We recollect that we have missed figures which were continually about a month ago. As we draw into the houses, so we draw a little more into ourselves. Winter lays its sober mantle over us as it does over the hills.

An aeroplane accident, when two men who, to avoid a crash, had attempted to bale out, were lost on the snowy moor, one for two days, one for ten, brought to the fells a modern tragedy which cast a shadow over the valley.

In November the damp made the cold worse to bear. You knew it was November by the spongy state of the green, which is not well drained. Looking out one morning we felt something missing in the scene, and saw that the seat had gone from its place. That marked a definite date in the country calendar, when we knew that summer had fled, and we must settle down to winter.

For three nights in succession the terrier scented a hedgehog in the thick grass at the side of the road. The third night he touched its spikes with a paw, and the cumbersome-looking creature darted out of the grass as nimbly as a rabbit, and travelled at a great speed down the road. It looked like a pavement-seller's toy running on wheels. We were reminded of how the first year we possessed the cottage Hardy scratched an opening into the hibernating quarters of a hedgehog, but we covered it up again, and its winter sleep did not seem to be disturbed.

On the morning of 5th November it was pathetic to see broken up a local museum which had been started almost a century ago. We bought a few bygones, chiefly because we felt that some should be retained in the dale into which they had been gathered with such enthusiasm. After the packhorse bells our most interesting purchase was a mulling pan, a cone-shaped copper pan which was pushed into the fire to warm ale. We are told that when Willie Metcalfe went into the Cat Hole Inn in

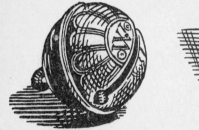
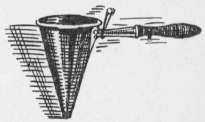

Packhorse Bell   *Mulling Pan*

Swaledale he walked to a certain hook, took down the mulling pan, thrust it into the fire, and called for some ale; he always carried cloves and sugar in his pocket to spice the brew. Sometimes an egg was added to the mixture. 'You ask old Tom about mulled ale,' said a farmer. 'He'd sup it till he slipped on his back.' Another purchase was a horn which used to be blown to call the cattle home near Semerwater.

The trees clinging to their leaves belied the season. The sycamores were the first to stand gaunt and naked, for their yellowing leaves were an easy prey to the wind. While the coppers and reds, golds and yellows of autumn grew daily more vivid in the gills, the ash-trees remained undaunted by the weather, until with another sudden frost the branches were bare, and the leaves a green carpet underneath them.   How Cobbett in his admiration of that tree would have approved of the numerous ashes in the dales.   'You will see the oak *shaved* up on the side of the breeze,' he says.   'But the ash stands upright as if in a warm, woody dell.   We have no tree that attains a greater height than the ash; and certainly none that equals it in beauty of leaf.' Many a bend of road or lane is made more lovely by a spreading ash-tree.   It is also one of the few trees that burn well when green.

The trees were leafless as we went up the valley to Raydale. The catkins which still clung to the sallows were seeding, and the fluff from them whirled in the air by the wind was like feathery snow.   The bleached winter garb of the hills made a fitting setting for the lake, which far below us broke into foam-edged waves on the shore.   We could see where a line of twigs and brushwood marked the height to which the water had risen in a previous storm.   Through Marsett, that hamlet where Jane Lambert, who sold the cottage in 1699, lived, we came to the lumber camp.

The autumn scene with the horses churning through mud was different from the summer days when their feet sank deep in dust.   The hill-sides were more denuded now; as far as we could see only a few weak saplings and the jagged trunks of small trees broken by the larger ones in their fall remained.   Outside the mill the sawdust heap, which could not be burnt because of the black-out, had now doubled itself in size.

As we returned we stood for a time where the highway which the Romans planned starts on its way over the fells.   It is a green track running between walls now, the one we see from the cottage windows, but the surface which the Romans made keeps it firm and hard.   Do we to-day find these tracks so thrilling because they have more affinity with our modern roads than any which came after them?   Our new highways cut the country as they do. Neither we nor the Romans are responsible for the rolling English road.

A small flock of fieldfares arrived, and fed in the Abbey Garth on the north.   The yellow wagtails, assembling there for flight, voraciously searched for insects under the noses of the cows. The high thorn hedge at the back of the garden was hung with bright red berries which remained while the leaves turned golden and began to drop. Then fieldfares and blackbirds and a pair of hedge sparrows raided it together, and for two days stuffed themselves in a frenzy which augured bad weather. That was before the snowstorm; when the brighter days came again the winter birds began to haunt the hedge. The breasts of the robins vied in colouring with the few berries that were left; wrens flitted in and out; great tits and blue tits darted above and through it and hung from the branches as they pecked. One blue tit perched on a cabbage under the north window, and seen against the green leaves its blue head reminded us of the colour of those autumn hills. So the thorn hedge in its sheltered nook is a playground and a working ground for the birds through the year. In it they find their green mansions.

The unusually cold weather made the more timid of the adult evacuees think regretfully of the sunny south and look for other quarters. A woman, evidently from one of the hamlets, asked in the grocer's shop if she was staying, replied: 'Aye, I'm sticking it out. We've been here all the summer, and a lot of them have gone back, but I'm sticking it out if I can.' She was wearing a tweed coat and blue slacks, which we noticed particularly because we have been mercifully free from those ugly sights all the summer.

One wonders what will be the final legacy left by the evacuees. In the long run the children will take away more than they give, but adults come with fixed habits and a certain sense of grievance. The very fact that they are evacuees also means that they come from towns and bring town ways and ideas. A child in a nearby village was found putting raspberry jam round her mouth with a spoon, and when asked by her mother what she was doing, she said: 'I'm making my lips like Mrs. Z.'s.'

As befits the importance of the place it has many shops, and our buying is divided among them. Although they can be differentiated as grocers', fancy shops, and stationers', yet all retain delightfully a semblance of the village shop which sells everything. You can buy draperies at the grocers' or groceries at the fancy shops. In spite of war they put on a festive Christmas air. Gay cards and calendars made up for the lack of quantity in other articles. Miss Banks sensibly kept an iron hand over her stock, and allowed no one to have an undue share, whilst she thought

regretfully of less restricted days.   We missed most the decorated
windows gaily lit.

In our turn we sent away the carol singers who came in November, but we welcomed them in December, for the youthful
voices were doubly precious when war had silenced the Christmas
bells and darkened the lights of cottage windows.   Before we
handed out the coppers after a verse of *Good King Wenceslas* we
followed the advice of a daleswoman, and asked the names of the
figures standing in the darkness, to guard against their becoming
nightly visitors.

One night Cuthbert, Arnold, and John came inside to sing their
carols.   They stood against the table under the old beams, and,
after getting over the difficulty of keeping straight faces, sang in
clear, sweet voices the peaceful familiar words of *When shepherds
watched their flocks by night*, *Away in a manger*, and the inevitable
Good King Wenceslas.   The spaniel sat looking up at them on the
rug, and when they had finished, after a little encouragement, he
threw back his head and sang himself.

Late one December afternoon we climbed the road to the moor.
Out on its open expanse it might have been any mild winter
day, for the moor keeps its garb unchanged from early autumn
until late spring.   Bleached grass, withered rushes and heather,
mingled in varying shades of brown which were restful and
satisfying.   We scarcely spoke until we turned homewards, and
then it was in the quiet tones which a stay on extensive upland
brings; there is no need to speak loudly in its thin atmosphere.

We talked of the year in which we had come to know the valley
better; of experiences which had been lovelier than any we had
hoped for; of new friends made.   Impressions of the summer
passed through our minds.   The processions of visitors we saw
now not as holiday-makers, but as hard-working citizens snatching
a few days' well-earned rest.   There came vividly a picture of one
of our friends, an observer in the Royal Air Force, who had loved
this moor over which we were walking.   He came with his wife
three times, and gave his enthusiasm to the cottage, the books,
the furniture; and then he was killed flying.   The war wiped out
his plans to record the parts of Yorkshire which he knew well and
decreed that other plans must remain unmade.

We realized how, with fewer cars on the roads, a peace and
quietness which we had almost forgotten permeated the valley.

The sense of speed and rush, of judging the day's outing by the mileage, had been absent. It was good to have Sunday as a time of rest and recuperation, to feel that on that day the village belonged to those who live in it and not to crowds of motorists.

We remembered how we had enjoyed working in the soil, growing things ourselves. And through every thought, like a theme song, was the water lapping on the shore of the tarn, in sunshine and greyness, with the coming and the going of the birds.

And what of the future? We cannot tell what changes another year will bring for us; but on the moor we ignored immediate uncertainties, and looked forward to a time when the guns are silent and no more bombs fall. What of the village in that time?

May it have its share in the lofty ideals and progressive schemes which will bring the new vigorous life to which we look forward. Its chief part in reconstruction will surely lie along the way of an increased and vital interest in the land. For the industrial areas there will be new towns, modern buildings, and lay-outs. The country's not unworthy role would seem to be to ensure that progress still preserves the old traditions for the generations that follow, particularly in places like our own whose traditions are worth preserving. It has no fringe of incongruous buildings, and surely having escaped so far it will never suffer it. The newly awakened pride in what we have come so near to losing will rise against the introduction of anything that jars. New buildings, if any are necessary, and reconstructions, will conform to the rest, and not be standardized boxes to take the magic from the scene. What is good in the new can be grafted on to the old, as has happened here since the seventeenth-century hall was built.

Gradually, as the sun disappeared from sight, the western sky was spread with a golden hue against which the hills stood out dark and velvety. A thin cerise line cut across it, and grew until it was a wide shaft. It was so bright and clear that it lit the valley. We could distinguish each village and hamlet, even the market town, by the pall of smoke which hung over it. A soft wind blowing down the dale carried with it a thin drift of smoke which lost itself in the haze over the next village; and so it continued eastward. It seemed a symbol of the life of the valley where each community is centred in itself, and yet influences the others.

Then in the dusk we were looking down to the roofs of the village with our own immediately below taking its place amongst the rest. A curl of smoke rose from the new chimney. We passed between the gateposts, lifted the latch, and entered the cottage. Peats thrown on to the glowing fire brought the scent of the moor into the room. We realized that the cottage had settled into a home, able to open its doors to new books, new treasures, new people. The name 'Coleshouse' had come to have a meaning again.